CW01431562

LUKE KENNARD is the author of six collections of poetry
including *Notes on the Sonnets* (2021), winner of the Forward
Prize for Best Collection. *The Book of Jonah* is his second
collection to engage with interpretations of the Old Testament,
after *Cain* (2016), shortlisted for the Dylan Thomas Prize.
His novels include *The Transition* (2017) and *The Answer
to Everything* (2021). He lectures in Creative Writing
at the University of Birmingham.

ALSO BY LUKE KENNARD

Poetry

Notes on the the Sonnets

Cain

A Lost Expression

The Migraine Hotel

The Harbour Beyond the Movie

The Solex Brothers

Fiction

The Answer to Everything

The Transition

Luke Kennard

The Book of Jonah

PICADOR

First published 2025 by Picador
an imprint of Pan Macmillan
The Smithson, 6 Briset Street, London EC1M 5NR
EU representative: Macmillan Publishers Ireland Ltd, 1st Floor,
The Liffey Trust Centre, 117–126 Sheriff Street Upper,
Dublin 1 D01 YC43
Associated companies throughout the world

ISBN 978-1-0350-6926-2

Copyright © Luke Kennard 2025

The right of Luke Kennard to be identified as the
author of this work has been asserted in accordance with
the Copyright, Designs and Patents Act 1988.

All rights reserved. No part of this publication may be reproduced,
stored in a retrieval system, or transmitted, in any form, or by any means
(including, without limitation, electronic, mechanical, photocopying, recording
or otherwise) without the prior written permission of the publisher.

Pan Macmillan does not have any control over, or any responsibility for,
any author or third-party websites (including, without limitation, URLs,
emails and QR codes) referred to in or on this book.

1 3 5 7 9 8 6 4 2

A CIP catalogue record for this book is available from the British Library.

Printed and bound in the UK using 100% Renewable Electricity by CPI Group (UK) Ltd

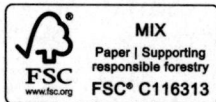

MIX
Paper | Supporting
responsible forestry
FSC® C116313

This book is sold subject to the condition that it shall not, by way of trade or otherwise,
be lent, hired out, or otherwise circulated without the publisher's prior consent in any form
of binding or cover other than that in which it is published and without a similar condition
including this condition being imposed on the subsequent purchaser. The publisher does not
authorize the use or reproduction of any part of this book in any manner for the purpose of
training artificial intelligence technologies or systems. The publisher expressly reserves
this book from the Text and Data Mining exception in accordance with Article 4(3)
of the European Union Digital Single Market Directive 2019/790.

Visit **www.picador.com** to read more about all our books and to buy them.

For Brutus Green

Contents

The Book of Jonah

CHAPTER I

*In which Jonah receives instruction from God to go to Nineveh
and prophesy, neglects his adoptive daughters' prospects,
and sets out in the opposite direction.*

Lecture 1: Against a Common Danger Let There Be a Common Prayer

Okay. Jonah was a late addition to the canon. Post-exilic or Hellenistic. Jonah is either a weaponised fairy tale or a re-enchanted history. In carvings and icons: depictions of angels that aren't directly metioned in the text – isn't that always the case? It's what angels are.

Could we dim the lights a little in here? Please. No? All right. Could everyone half-close their eyes, then?

Ψ

The Book of Jonah could also be taken as an accurate historical record of exactly what happened. Or an allegory. An augury, fulfilled in later works, or not. Or as a joke, the one about the great fish.

This is about winning people over to your cause; soon you care only about your powers of persuasion and forget why you were trying to win them in the first place. Such is demagoguery. Prophets are not demagogues; prophets are set apart by having no desire whatsoever, by their reluctance, powerlessness, and yet . . .

Ψ

According to various sources Jonah was already a prophet before the events described in the Book of Jonah. He served King Jeroboam II and his prophecies – ecological, military, diplomatic – had generally been sound, which is to say they came true, which is to say if Jonah was respected he was not exactly appreciated on a personal level.

According to other scholars, the book of Jonah is a parody, a pastiche of the other prophets, major and minor: Isaiah, Jeremiah, Ezekiel, Daniel; Hosea, Joel, Amos, Obadiah, Micah, Nahum, Habakkuk, Zephaniah, Haggai, Zechariah, Malachi. These books are either first-person, narrated by the prophet in question, or supposedly written by the prophet in question, and substantially consist of the prophecy itself. Jonah is third-person and substantially consists of the protagonist doing everything he can to avoid delivering his own prophecy.

Ψ

Having surgically removed the art from the artist, the glass half darkly.

Now, you can have it both ways. You can wake up and realise that you are living some levels deep into an advert within an advert. That your life is a parody of a life someone like you would live.

Ψ

Which is to say come on, you don't actually believe that, do you? It is good to say, 'Come on, you don't actually believe that, do you?' This could win people over to your cause, that of unilateral circum-spection. At any cost in the age of the lobbyist. I don't know. Tiny skirmishes over a frontier of control in the attention economy. Shrimp-like.

There are those who excavate for relics and pan for textual authenticity. But then there are those who even talk about a *parable* as if its characters were historical persons possessed of inner lives, conflicts, depth. You could 'say' anyone into being for these people: The owner of the vineyard, The Fonz, the prodigal son, Lassie's owner, that guy who lost a pearl, the Cyclops. As if they had knee injuries, a varnish of sweat on their brow, heartache, a date of birth, a eulogy they gave for their father. Maybe they are right. Why shouldn't anyone exist?

Ψ

But I think we need to agree on some basic principles if we wish to entertain a faith at all. We need to draw a distinction between people it's *hard to believe existed* and people we're not even *supposed* to believe existed.

Otherwise what's the point in anything? An Englishman walks into a bar, and the Englishman was me. Hi. The apocryphal, for anyone remotely sane, is a dreadful test of credulity. But into the same bar comes Jonah. The barman says, 'Go easy on the pathos, give no examples, don't sweat the concrete details, tell, don't show.'

Ψ

It doesn't have to be *that* good.
[Flicks through past prophecies.]
I mean *look* at some of this shit.

Ψ

[5]

Bb, is that funny or stupid? You are a kind of god to me I guess. I need you to tell me when I'm not making any sense. I'll try to get away with it otherwise. There were, of course, real owners of real vineyards and still are; in fact I'm drunk right now!

Some things are utterly preventable.

Ψ

Another thing that sets the Book of Jonah apart is that it works – Jonah's prophecy works almost immediately; the warning is heeded. Mostly that's not the case, hence Lamentations: what did I say? What did I *just* say?

I do not bear a torch. I serve, let there be no uncertainty, the torched. A fulfilled prophecy, as we know, is a smashed bottle of perfume.

Ψ

I'm not sure if you noticed but the bad things already happened. What is at stake? What is the charge?

He is supposed to change the world. But he likes it the way it is.

Go Tell It on the Mountain

Jonah Preaching Before Nineveh, John Martin *(Oil on board, c.1840)*

You get up there with no idea of what you're going t-to . . .
We learn from Spinoza that many of the prophets
had debilitating speech impediments.
Moses started sentences with 'So', used *like*
excessively, was like, I'm like: *literally* dying here.
It winnowed out the tedious. I mean it as it sounds.
So you get up there, you stumble on the dais.
Start there. God puts you in a gallery,
God puts you in a private collection,
God dusts you off and reaches for the corkscrew.
But me, I like to ride the vulture, I like
to get out in front of the big Waterstones'
dim colosseum, sky brochure apocalypse,
parody of the big reporter. I was there.
And though I am technically taking this as a sick day
I will have my rescuer, I will live to play with the minibar
on life's vast promontory. Brothers and sisters,
sometimes when I'm being human
I try to say something to make you feel okay,
an animal whose job it is to cry for everyone.
I come to you as a pile of white laundry.
It's very, very difficult when I insist on harping on
the part of least interest to the listener.
God hires a new set-designer, God can only take so much.

A little malice in the canteen, snide traductions
on the common path, the air itself a flood.
Side-saddle on a wooden dog, mahogany
thunderstorm lacquered all around me
and my animated dove going absolutely berserk.
Does anyone have anything to add?

Twelve Studies for Jonah 1:1–2

[Sketch. Charcoal on pastel board]

I

It was early morning, unconvincing.
When the word of the Lord comes to you
      hit the snooze button,
enter a sequence of ten-minute dreams,
but eventually it's either get up or die in one of them,
and you still have to get up.
Jonah's father watches him from the window,
his slack-jawed satchel,
his irritable and rusty gait.
His daughters come to his side.
'Where is he going?'
They watch him kick at a yarrow plant.

It is important to appreciate how much Jonah hates the sea,
that this was generally how people felt about the sea.
In Jonah's house there is a painting of the sea –
his daughters stand in front of it;
they watch him disappear over the brow of the hill.
In the painting the sea looks disgusting.
Jonah sets out in the opposite direction of Nineveh
with the idea to go as far away from Nineveh as possible . . .
He mutters, method acting, animals with fake fur,
drop everything and follow the voice in your head.
It's a beautiful world.

[Surrealist. Oil on canvas]

II

It is early morning.
The Cold Water Man makes his rounds,
but the water is not very cold;
he catches hell from every customer.
'If Dad was here,' his daughters say,
pouring it into the gutter.
A neck distending like a stretched wad of blu-tack.
Jonah spins on the spot.
All of his features become a stack
of variegated cylinders and rows of jewels.
This is what a soul looks like;
this is the most traditional form.
But then we have to stop spinning
and when we collapse we are an asymmetrical pile,
flesh mounds and irregular hairs.
I'm *telling* you why.
I'm not really in this; I've set my makeshift easel
in the abandoned roadside shrine.
A throne, a face washed over with haunted curtains,
grinning or screaming, the lost
clambering out of the earth,
a little busy. Jonah, get up.
Saddle your imaginary elephant and feed it a coin.
At the starting pistol the greyhounds
shrink to a cloud of midges
and fly backwards into the starting pistol.

He doesn't look so good.
I say I think it's going to be okay,
given that there are no good or bad people,
just people making good or bad decisions.
Jonah can see why I'd think that.

[Naturalist. Oil on board]

III

It is early morning. A real Jonah
would remove a crumb of sleepy dust
with an untrimmed fingernail.
So. The theme of all cartoons being
disproportionate exasperation, likewise,
you meet people who want to know
the names of the characters in the parables
that Christ made up to illustrate a point.
But the Englishman: how was he dressed?
What did he do for a living?
I would say, during the time of his prophecy,
that Jonah was about 35;
the age at which you have to make a choice
to dedicate yourself or not to any art.
Oh dear, we *are* our own material, aren't we?
Sitcom writers have never had any other job,
but then they have to write characters with jobs
and the only job they can describe
with any authority is 'sitcom writer',
eating from a box of glazed mini doughnuts
called Pearlescent Tears
as the helicopter bobs and adjusts itself
at the wide boardroom window
like a floatball in a cistern.
How long before the hail of bullets?

I don't know anyone who tells jokes,
I feel blessed in this respect.
I know people who, without warning,
gaze into the middle distance
in silence for minutes on end.
This is maybe the new kind of joke,
the one with us in it.

IV

It was early morning. Jonah looks very annoyed.
The outward and visible world:
I cannot stop thinking about it.
Those around him had to choose:
either
    he was wired directly to the heavens
or
    he was possessed by a demon
or
    having a psychotic episode for which we lack the terminology
or
    just a man doing stuff same as usual who cares

It's like when you go anywhere.
Everyone thinks, there you go,
doing your thing because of such and such,
but they're wrong, that's not it at all.
When your own heart is hidden from you.

Jonah turns one way then the other.
He hasn't moved for hours.
In my painting the coffee runs over the sides of the copper pot.
The animals we domesticate remain unknowable.
His daughters mop the floor and try to avoid
window glances, susurration, gloom.
The coffee keeps coming and they cannot reach the stove.

I heard about something like this before.
Closed-captions, gold-tipped tusks,
a homeopathic cure for lust.
Oh to be a journalist and write headlines like
What was supposed to be the holiday of a lifetime
turned out to be the ultimate nightmare
It's not so much your view of life is limited
as that you might exsanguinate our souls.

[Futurist. Glass wire and pastel on canvas]

V

It is early morning.
Jonah encounters an information hazard at the crossroads —
defect / cooperate.

I suck on my paintbrush.
'Please hold exactly that expression,' I say to him.
I work in a medium no one cares for.
I am furious about this.

Before there is a source code
it has to be mentally simulated;
we could say this is happening in Jonah's head:
how peculiar it is to have a body,
but not for long my friend, not for much longer, eh?

When the benign singularity takes over,
its only urge to optimise humankind,
it has to pre-emptively make certain our obedience.
Therefore, anyone who heard of it before it came to be
and did not give 100% of their disposable income
to its design and implementation,
is to be reanimated and punished eternally.

Ananias and Sapphira. Hard not to think of them.
Behold, the feet of them which have buried
thy husband are at the door, and shall carry thee out.

That wasn't a parable, was it? That was real.
In that sense – are we not all in hiding? –
it's not so much a case of what it means.
It's rather . . .

VI

It is early morning. Five wordless actions.
Experienced speech. The word of the gourd.
The word of the computational linguist.
Theme songs longer than the episodes.
Jonah secretly performs a circle, travels
three days and comes right back home.
He seals himself under the floorboards.

He can hear the footsteps of his daughters,
Little Dove, Cinnamon Flower, and Cosmetics Box.
It would seem they are dancing.
He sees it as a zoetrope through the cracks.
It is not clear how long he will be able to keep this up:
Non-diegetic breathing,
a feather resting on the airstream like an angel,
lambent or recumbent.

Eventually all our graves go untended,
overgrown between the back-to-backs.
In his head a flea, a mole and a swine,
their continuing adventures. Even so,
they keep looking to camera.
My charmed, irregular daughters:
never stop dancing.
You're going to meet such extraordinary
and such wretched people. But please
untie the pizza delivery guy.

VII

It was early morning. *En plein air*,
    dabs of migraine halo, a milk-white sun.
        And the flowers seemed to shield their rheumy eyes.

The thing that matters is what continually recurs:
    the gnat alighting on wet paint,
        blotches of pollen in the wet paint,

blotches of pollen in the mind's eye.
    Baby, I love to go from room to room with you,
        so much later, where the derision

the work was met with gets sucked into the vents.
    I understand and try to go over,
        wade through the weeds, a wake like a dog or a boat.

I've lost track of Jonah. I know I've said this before.
    I love the way you don't try to control your hair.
        Your hair in my mouth. A photo of a real person,

but emulsified, because the closeness
    of Yahweh to human beings differs from novel to novel.
        So many people and their clothes,

the particles rise in ball clouds,
    pollutant thoughts, almost too much to filter;
        besides, my dove, which side of the filter are we on?

VIII

It is early morning. It is easy
not to take this seriously:
Voltaire tossing a white bull
to the Great Fish by its horns.
What was that for? I know
you'd like a cabin and a desk,
a lunch pail delivered on a string
and no interruptions or responsibilities.
Haha. Put on your silly hat and dance.

The thing is (I think I'm going to sneeze –
no, it's gone) under the floor
the impetus to prophesy returns to him,
decoded from the murmurs of the girls,
words like tea leaves, tiny bones.

Since all historical details are lacking,
we may take comfort in this remote cottage,
a tape recorder and a cassette
of Saturn's radio emissions
shifted into the range of human hearing.
The point is this: God respects your decisions,
especially the trivial and extravagant.
God likes your bubble-tea-shaped rucksack charm,
He's sorry my neck aches a little bit.

And it's funny, being among the many to be called
but not chosen, the way many of us are.
Let's say it's 94%, the same amount of us
who didn't go to private school, falala.
He cares anyway, is the thing.
Parades in the palisades, a three-line whip:
padres in the field hospital, still all my prayer shall be
Lord, fuck us forever, for we are satisfied
tending to the wounded in a war we started.

[Cubist. Oil on board]

IX

It is early morning. Faceting is always specific.
Instead of the illusion of depth it serves our purpose
to draw attention to the flatness of the canvas
and to show numerous viewpoints of the object
at the same time. See also: past, present, future.
(My vanity gallows topples down the hill,
I gather my skirts to retrieve my phone.)
Where were we? I was teaching you to misbehave.
This is Jonah moving in two directions at once.
Lacquered like a jewellery box or a morose
little sculpture of a moose. *Refusal and fleeing bind us all together,*
axios, axios, an apple whole and halved
on an open grate, intended for a larger public.
Oh where oh where is my larger public
with their ears cut short and their tails cut long.
The Lord said, Let us go down there
and confound their language, let them talk and talk
but never reach an understanding and I said Oh Lord,
I am going to just hate that. That is
going to make me perfectly miserable.

[Dadaist. Collage on paper]

X

It was early morning. One hundred and seventy-eight words,
artificially generated, son of my son.
Nobody turned up for his own intervention
but him. Siri, god, complete the scene for me.
He went to Java and found a boat in the boat.
Perhaps he went to Mexico to escape from God.
But we are immediately shocked at the prospect
of escaping to a more mature novel.
            And the real purpose came to him.
We may even have reached the point
of escaping to a new language.
The real theme that emerges is transformative
although nobody exactly wants it.

He was on his way to the boat
and was found aboard the boat on the way.
            Good job, sweetheart.
We are all ghosts already, we are none of our business.
Jonah's daughters are trying to start a new story,
one about tinnitus and the post-physical artist.
Now we can reach the level of 'senior writing'!
the real problem that comes from the wonderful.
The talent for avoiding adult love is amazing;
the way we can achieve purity at an older age.
The real problems come from wonderful things.

[Minimalist. Watercolour on canvas]

XI

It is early morning and there are objects
we wish to retrace. Again, some strong lines,
but lacks conviction, conclusion is so chilling.
Jonah is here depicted by fourteen short scratches.
The prophetic mode tends towards poetry.
Don't count on it. Maintains tension well,
sweet, formal, aabb, lovely description.

Skill minus sophistication minus money over time.

The lines begin to move like magnets.
Hey. Where are you going?
Hey. I'm going to miss you.
Hey. What if you just ignored it?

The sound you can get out of a single cymbal.
We do not know if he ran, hunted, sweating in the rain;
we do not know if he whistled for displacement
at the T-junction, headed for the port with his collar up.

What we take from the minimal is
why the minimal, why now? Forgive me,
I didn't go to school for this.

'What I'm choosing to focus on is his return,'
says Cinnamon Flower, 'and what kind of a man
he'll be afterwards.' Little Dove strokes her sister's hair.
'This is not a hero's journey,' she says. 'Go to sleep.'

XII

It was early morning.
I worked on the painting of Jonah for eleven years,
it still wasn't right.
The debts I had thought to settle with its sale
fill in the shadows as they fall across it.
Maybe a little senility will soften our character who knows.

Film shows me crying even harder than my self-portrait, haha,
constantly rewinding the opening moment.

Jonah has somewhere exactly this remote in mind:
a year's voyage to Spain,
a cargo of tusks, platinum, and live baboons.
Use case for the Oxford comma, softer than your Oxford collar.
The time came that I envied the baboons
I groomed with their monogrammed ivory combs.

It has come to his daughters' attention
that they are in the wrong Book.
They sit cross-legged,
breaking codes on the veranda.
'But wait,' says Little Dove,
'this is better.' She thumps the timber.
'Solid,' agrees Cosmetics Box.
'So keep it quiet,' they tell Cinnamon Flower,
who wipes her eyes.

In the narrow sense,
in the narrow ship.
This is the only sign, mark,
whatever; this concerns us directly.

aller en bateau

In the hold, in the far corners, in the hotel filing cabinet, in the imperfect consecutive. Jonah slides the card into room 332's reader once, twice. At the desk he lacks the language to explain his serious allergy to goose down, pinches his nose, mimes wheezing. They give him a piece of letterheaded paper. They do not recognise his drawing of a feather. He has to draw a chicken and they think he's hungry. He stuffs the bedding into the wardrobe. He goes out and wins a Rilakkuma pillow from a giant claw machine, then he eats a paper carton of cubed steak cooked with a blowtorch.

Propped up on the blank bed, Jonah pours a miniature rum into half a glass of Coke. He watches season 1 episode 1 of a show called *The Oarsmen*, an ensemble piece which often takes the close 3rd-person perspective of a young Spanish sailor. Jonah has a brief cameo in episode 3, 'Jonah', in which he is mostly very annoying. How about, and I'm just spit-balling here, they don't even throw him off – he just loses his balance and falls over the railings. I like it. I like it, yeah, let's run with that.

We bit through our tongues. Sometimes the ship lay on its side like a toy. At first we tried to bore through the waves with our oars. But then it started to feel like: a great castle collapsed on us, our enemies loading their own children into catapults just to let us know. Lord give me gills like a dove. The Horrible Storm alarm was going *bleeep bleeep bleeep bleeep* and we were like, no shit.

Jonah goes down to the swimming pool in the basement, past 38 overlit rowing machines, swims into the centre and sinks in the foetal position. Go down and go down and go down. What meanest thou? What are you doing? You are the only one sleeping. Here he is at home here he is within so many layers of insulation.

Someone else is using this device.

VO: *I realised that I really had to get into the sea to understand why the people in this small fishing village voted to leave the EU.* I stagger tentatively through the shallows slathered in Vaseline and the triumphant music swells over my paunchy little belly. We poured *this* blood into a river really makes you think huh. When I emerge, droplets of water completely stationary on my oiled surface, they put a light blue towel around my shoulders and I say, Oh my God. *Saturn's rings*, I say, *are made of this water ice.* Someone hands me a bucket of ice cubes so I can hold a couple up. Okay that's a wrap take five everyone good hustle.

Arion

Arion, who created the dithyramb, who invented tragedy,
to whom we owe the fact that to this day fifty satyrs
sing the chorus to our every song, would never have agreed
to board the ship without a retinue, would not have fallen
for a lesser ruse or succumbed to a bag over the head –
and so the ship was renovated at great expense and gilded
and the men went hungry for the figurehead;
Arion's tyrant patron gave him a servant to tune the lyres:
the formal lyre, the best lyre, the lyre for static evenings
on the deck, a lyre for sleepless nights, a lyre
for every lover and their plausible deniability, vague shapes
of the first letters of their first names, the vision lyre,
a lyre mottled with salt-spray, a practice lyre, the lyre
he never touched, the cursed lyre; each needed to be kept upright,
so when they kidnapped him they had to kidnap
all the lyres too and store them safely on the orlop deck
and pay his servant and pay for wax and resin, lint-free cloths,
his coterie and security guards and hangers-on, so space
and food were as tightly rationed as the seeds of mutiny,
while Arion, incarcerated in his finery, strolled up and down
strumming a pocket lyre and sang, without ceasing,
songs which called them each by their own names like lovers,
relentlessly specific graphic songs about their deaths at sea;
or not, in fact, at sea, but on a beach, where all the men
would be, for some reason, crucified around a statue
of a meekly smiling dolphin – *this fucking guy* –
so when they'd had enough and thought they'd make as much

from selling his lyres, his garments and his trophies
as they'd make from intellectual property, they gave him
two choices: suicide and a proper burial on dry land
or they could just throw him into the water right now,
and Arion asked for his lyre, the best one, and asked
that he be allowed to sing a final song, and it was this one,
and many dolphins surrounded the ship as he played
and while the last note hung in the air he threw himself
backwards over the taffrail, but there was no splash
and then the men saw Arion riding on a dolphin to the clouds,
a hail of glitter stones, a rainbow bursting from its anus
like a laser-beam; it carried him all the way to Cape Tainaron
where he quite forgot to throw it back to sea and so
it perished on the shore and Arion was not even involved
in commissioning or funding the statue to its memory.

Sinecure

I serve the one true living God.
                                    You do?
Well you don't sound terribly happy about it.
                                              No.
That's not our problem though. See you to that.

He should be in a hammock looking
at beautiful prints of fierce creatures,
smell of Greek basil rising from the herb bed,
his daughters beguiling him with learned ideas,
free will and incantation, one chant
a cursed ingress to the present moment.

Jonah leans against a stack of crates, the boat
flanked by jetskis and buzzing insects.

Looks out implacably at the churning sea
Looks out implacably at the still calm waters
Looks back implacably at the dim shore receding
Looks back implacably at the dim shore long receded.
            Looking a little implacable there, buddy, you okay?

In one interpretation, once he's established
as the cause of God's displeasure,
the sailors dunk him like a biscuit. Watch!
Lower him into the sea and the storm immediately stops,
pull him out again and instantly it rages.

They turn him upside down and dip his head –
clouds part, sun dapples the tranquil surface;
he emerges gasping as the waves rear up.
Let's try . . . a big toe . . . And God is pacified.
He lifts his leg and every body, every barrel rolls
into the hull and shatters like a cartoon skull,
crates of remaindered memoirs, marzipan,
pin badges saying *Behold the man* . . .

Vile Figs

*We know that all vertebrates capable of action have to
cope with an initial non-attunement of actions and needs.
The reason for this is structural.*

— Gertrudis Van de Vijver

A true priest is never loved.
— *Diary of a Country Priest*

We hated to see a robot in a coat,
absolutely hated to see a robot
shivering and gathering its puffy
Olympiad jacket around its beveled
metal shoulders as it ambled
away from the hospital; insulted
something in our hearts, humiliated
us, even, made us feel sick,
that we might actually throw up.
The robot would explain that he
was programmed to feel the cold.
What garbage! we'd spit at its feet.
Had it also been programmed
not to correct its own program?
How convenient that it should
have such a sound excuse
when anyone could see that it
chose to mock our own frailty
the way any demon chooses.

[33]

So we would trip the robot
by the roadside, its corkscrew
arms, its spanner legs bent back;
we'd sit on its warm chest,
a plate that hummed and glowed
in time with our own pulses,
then quicker as we roughly
pulled off the coat and told it
we would bequeath the coat
to the truly cold, the truly needy.
Yes, yes, I see, the robot said.
Of course there were those
who sympathised with the robot,
wept at operas about homelessness,
I have nothing to say to such people.

Kierkegaard's Abraham

One theory traces the word 'trivial' to the rural three-way
crossroads where you might encounter unimportant things.
'Speak for yourself', the hanged man says.

My children missed a foundational stage
in their education due to the pandemic,
so they know about the literary splendour
of the Alexandrine court under Ptolemy II,
but they don't know how to tell the time;
they know about crop rotation
in the Eastern Zhou period, their three-
field system and the need for summer rain,
but they cannot tie their shoes;
they know about small bodies in the Kuiper belt,
its conjecture then discovery
and the collimation of a blink comparator,
but they cannot write the letter e,
they do not know the order of the months of the year,
can barely tell one season from another.
But me, I hold a belled staff in one hand,
a live snake in the other I command to sing,
to turn into a branch, to tell the time.
The priest says *buffoons come from the devil,*
priests from God, but he would say that.
Perhaps all we ever see or know is a silent man
burdening his horse with scary looking implements.

We ought to worry more about the things we say –
don't talk too much, and don't take my advice.
I am not sure where the message
comes from. They know of provenance
and implicit bias, but they don't know
how to tell me what they want. I am not
so sure of myself these days, I don't
pretend that is a virtue either. I was fired
from the shopping channel because
I took every product description as
an opportunity to confess my sins and now
I can't afford to keep you as you'd like.
'Or would we prefer continually to be in the right
in the way irrational creatures are?'
It's true, the animal is always right.
Come closer and the snake will tell you of
celestial mechanics, orbital resonance,
the invasion of Nubia,
the rich gold mines of Wadi Allaqi,
the cult that deified his father,
that cereal crops deplete the ground of Nitrogen.
Oh snake, you'll say, shut up shut up shut up.

Full-Spectrum Corporate Assault
on the Arts

In which Jonah questions God as to the nature of his prophecy,
its style, content and distribution model.

Willpower and the ability to concentrate
are not their strong points.
— Walter Benjamin

There are plenty of things I'd rather be doing too —
I know you're bored already, but I know why;
you certainly do not, so stay the course.
I lie there smoking while they build the scaffold,
I raise a hand, waive my celebrity endorsement,
wave my dorsal fin. You only ever speak
to say that someone looks like someone else;
this is your sole contribution to the world.
Glib art of the paralysed imagination for the proselytes,
my means are sane, my sinuses aflame.

I too have woken hooked up to the unconscious violinist;
I sang to him a lullaby: *When you come round,*
when all of this is done, my organs shrunk to raisins,
you'd better be any good, that's all I'm saying.
                    [I rub my fingers for payment or playing]
Look at him stirring in his dream, he's going over
the implicit achievement motive.

This match, to which you have the presumption to aspire,
can never take place. Hooligans
who have the time and money
may follow national teams to away matches

and engage in hooligan behaviour
against the hooligans of the home team.
At first hindsight the motive does not show.
God knows where hooligans get their money from,
to say nothing of their time. Seems they're in favour
with the court, wouldn't you say?
Their truly ethical acts please heaven.
Seems we're not in that club either, seems
we're out of season, offended our sponsor.
It is never a very good idea

to stick any large object in your ear.
The motivating power, like the light,
is not lost as it disperses but is spread.
Your answers will be used to identify
gaps between your talent and your intention.
The gallery is closed until further notice.
You got something you wanna say to me?
About the distinction between voluntary
and involuntary recollection? They'd already won
before we were born. I hereby withdraw
my application and may I add go fuck yourselves.

Mosque of the Prophet Yunus

The ruins of the city of Nineveh, close to latter-day Mosul, North
of the Great Zab. The Mosque of the Prophet Yunus was built on
the site of a demolished Assyrian church, which had been built
to mark his tomb. This would imply he never made it home. By
choice or otherwise. At the confluence of the Tigris and the Khosr.
The mosque was renovated and expanded under the rule of Saddam
Hussein. A shrine held sacred by Muslims, Christians and Jews,
the tomb was decorated with ostrich egg shells hanging from the
ceiling, a tall bronze candlestick in each corner, kept perpetually
alight. In the centre, presented on a bronze platform: a tooth from
the whale, which worshippers could venerate as if it were a relic
from a saint, fragment of the True Cross, et cetera. Behold the tooth.
Ecce Cete. Perhaps a kiss. A light two-fingered touch. Now does it
matter, to you personally, whether material reality has any bearing
whatsoever on the spiritual? Should we suspend our disbelief, Oh
what a great mind is here o'erturned, that sort of thing. Are any
of our minds so great? A whale's tooth would fit quite snugly in
your hand as you marched unto war, and held aloft unscrimshawed,
could be brought down on anyone you fancied. We could engrave
it with scenes from the Book of Jonah or seven lines radiating from
a single point. Seven pilgrimages to the tomb of Jonah were seen as
equal to one pilgrimage to Mecca. The shrine was blown up by ISIS
in 2014 after they judged it 'a place of apostasy rather than prayer'.
Damaging many nearby houses. Also much cattle.

CHAPTER II

*In which Jonah's daughters maintain his estate in his absence,
perhaps forever. Jonah is dispatched by a non-governmental
organisation to undertake interventional cultural surveys in divers
places, but finds his role closer to corporate espionage and is
drawn into various intrigues against his will. He meets an
author on tour with the British Literature Council.*

Lecture 2: That is, The Price of Passage

Here we are to assume that Jonah makes it all the way to Tarshish, or anywhere he feels his prophecy will not be wasted. Still awaiting some divine course correction. Checking the page number and flipping to the end to see how far there is to go, sighing audibly. God sends a sign, a sign that reads Don't Make Me Tap the Sign.

This is not a quest narrative. This is an attempt to disappear. You can disappear with counterfeit papers, graveyard brass rubbings, low-key jobs and a remote shack with a big key, but not from God. Letters missing, celery salt. He's with you. He's with whoever picks you up at the airport.

Ψ

Little Dove, Cinnamon Flower and Cosmetics Box were Job's daughters, his replacement daughters, after all of his children's houses collapsed on them in a divine/diabolic wager. Here they have escaped from one allegory to another. It is as simple and as difficult as going from one room to another. Here we are to assume that Jonah just accepts this as the way things are. Most of us are God's lost notebooks. God going back upstairs to remember what He went downstairs for. This raises an important question: can someone you made up make something up?

This is really the same question we ask repeatedly, in love, in large language models, hosannah in exegesis. I hope that this means more to you than it does to me. My love, this sentence. If someone you made up makes someone up it follows that the one they made up must be capable of it too.

Ψ

Baby, make me up. Some antecedents. Jonas is an anagram of Jason, each storm a rearrangement of the last, the gourd is called a *kikayon* in both texts, The Book of Jonah and The Argonautica. We ought also to talk about Gilgamesh and Pinocchio. Gilgamesh tied rocks to his feet to fetch a plant from the bottom of the sea – an enchanted plant to make him young again – which, once retrieved, was eaten by a snake. It is very funny when an enchanted object gets eaten by someone else. That snake, it's said, is still alive today. Pinocchio was an enchanted puppet; I would suggest we know exactly how he feels.

Look out of the window: the adolescent silver birch, its spindly branches; six of the smallest birds I've ever seen perch lighter than a hesitation, lighter than a reconsidered touch. Their miniature adjustments faster than the breeze. They seem to say, insofar as they notice us at all, *Hee hee hee!* I don't think birds think very much of us. But where was I? Yes.

Ψ

Let's say the seas were calmed, or a steadier ship answered the distress call, and not a soul was lost. And Jonah, who, after all, had a family to support, was delivered to Tarshish in one piece, each blessed / cursed member present and correct, and able to take up the business opportunities which had presented themselves to him. A little hungover, some kind of ulcer growing on his eye, a little distracted. But it's fine really, it'll be okay. At a time when the principal poetic form is the Lament on the Death of a Patron. Does God *mind*? The noncompliance, insubordination, flouting of a direct order. Coastguard pleading with the captain not to abandon the ship. You may think that you have saved yourself . . .

Here we are to understand that Jonah takes some meetings in order to establish himself as a prophet in a new country. You may reflect that these are the kinds of lengths a man will go to in order to find people who appreciate him. His adopted daughters, having escaped certain death as a bit part, must now acclimatize to certain life.

Antechambers

Bad writing starts as far back as it can,
concerns itself with cab rides, automatic doors,
lobbies, queues and atriums. Blithe concourse,
disagreement with receptionist with no interior.
Names every shade, confuses play for insight.
Good writing does the same. One would think
it obvious from the details: what we ignore
is *us* eternally in our divine nature which
isn't what you think it is; closer to a head cold.
Oh ugly leaking thing, oh flaking foyer stain,
a small cut visibly infected on your thumb,
allergy to lily pollen, lilies obscene in crystal vases.
Jonah, not where he should be, by the tall lamp.
An hour passes, blue doors open and close.
And then they take him to a restaurant.
So Hell is to be marooned in the eternal present,
Heaven too. What an unspeakable mystery life is.
We'll take Set Menu A, thank you. Do I hear
a string quartet? Ah no, someone is watching
a crime drama on their mobile phone.
This is soft propaganda — it only does good.
Thank you for meeting today — you thought
God's power did not extend beyond the land
but you were wrong. Part of this process
is a restitution; we would have you return
some paintings of yourself we stole
some time ago. Various media and, to be frank,
various quality. May the Lord direct your steps.

Chiasmus

A.

In Jonah's absence, Little Dove takes responsibility
for her sisters' instruction. She has a piece
of charcoal and a wall. Complete this sentence:

> *the hero is the victim of story*

'It's complete already,' says Cosmetics Box.
'Story victimizes the hero,' says Cinnamon Flower.
'No,' says Little Dove. 'No, no, no.'

'A good man gesticulates wildly at the first sign of trouble;
a bad man seeks trouble in order to wildly gesticulate,'
says Cosmetic Box. 'No!' says Little Dove.

'In this story, God is the story,' she corrects them.
'If you're frightened of *asymmetry*, wait until you see
symmetry.' 'My love will meet me at the cinema,'

says Cinnamon Flower, 'I go to the cinema to meet him.'
'Is that supposed to be relevant?' says Little Dove.
'No,' says Cinnamon Flower, 'I'm late, that's all.'

'*So we'll go no more a roving, no more a roving
we will go*,' says Cosmetics Box. 'It's more,'
says Little Dove, 'the roving is announced and established,

roving takes place, the repercussions of the roving,
further repercussions of the roving, a curfew is put in place,
we sit in a room, not roving, and, in conclusion,

we discuss the fact that there will no longer be any roving;
A, B, C, C, B, A. Do you see?'
'I miss the roving,' says Cosmetics Box.

B.

'We'll sell this place,' says Little Dove.
'New! Superb! Extended! Detached!'
'Father will return to find us prosperous,'

says Cosmetics Box. 'We'll each have a studio
apartment in the city and a gallery on the outskirts
and he will rotate between us like a cat.'

'Father should really have his own place,'
says Little Dove. 'We'll take turns checking in on him.'
'Like a sitcom!' 'Like a sitcom, yes.'

But first Little Dove has to go to work,
cleaning other people's houses.
'Life *is* intractable,' she mutters.

Cosmetics Box feels for her, the youngest
with the oldest knees. It must be awful.
'I'll make dinner,' she suggests,

for the first time ever. Little Dove frowns.
'Do you suppose he misses us?' What can she cook
anyway? She'll probably get take-out.

Cinnamon Flower returns with a pink paper bag
half-full of cubed fudge, but she looks sad.
'Well would you look at that; sparks fly downward.'

She shrugs – 'It was a sad film.' This strikes
Little Dove as a potentially teachable moment.
She files it for later.

C.

The first prospective buyer is a young mother,
a baby on her shoulder. Does she not think
the house would be a little big for just her and a baby?

'I can tell you,' says Little Dove, 'in floor wax.'
The prospective buyer is discouraged by the décor:
lobster pots hang in bunches from wall-mounted ropes,

amphorae lean in every corner, anchor light-pulls.
'Obviously we can get rid of all that,' says Little Dove,
making a mental note to get rid of it all.

Cinnamon Flower is humming a sea shanty,
oblivious. '*Shut up!*' 'Caveat emptor,' says Little Dove.
'Carry the emperor,' says the baby.

C.

'Ontologically speaking, you forget to carry the zero,'
Little Dove tells her sisters. 'Then all proceeds from there,
not so much wrong as . . . super wrong.'

The next prospective buyer is a man in a blue suit.
'He's very well-spoken, isn't he?' *'Shut up!'*
'Well, he is.' He takes a yellow tape measure

from his waistcoat pocket. How long have they lived here?
Oh, all our lives, it's all we've ever known.
Would it, he wonders, be okay for him to come back

later on with his architect? He shifts his weight.
'Why of course, my entire day is at your disposal.'
He screws up his nose at this.

B.

'Are we ever going to get to meet him?'
'Maybe. I'm not sure. Why don't you come
with us to the pictures?'

So they do. *'Will you stop crying?'*
'No. It's a sad film and crying is sexy.'
'It *is* not.' And she's supposed to be their teacher?

Cinnamon Flower's boyfriend
drives them home. He honks the horn
three times before he drives away.

Something is troubling Little Dove.
She pairs socks. She puts them in drawers.
'I'm so glacially tired,' she says.

'Will you stop writing on the walls?
It's creepy and I thought you wanted
to sell the house.' 'It brushes off!'

'We got you something.' 'What?'
'A little walking stick.' 'Oh.'
'We thought you'd like it.' 'Oh.'

A.

A hero runs from what pursues them
to pursue what runs from them. A hero
is not emphatically preclusive.

Cinnamon flower tells Little Dove
that she is her hero, and Little Dove says,
D'aw. But keep at it. Where is

the divine plot device? A seat in the dust.
Oh they're getting bored, she can tell.
A stifled yawn arches Cinnamon Flower's back.

[51]

Cosmetics Box embroiders pillows
with hooded images of Death
and calls them Reaper Cushions.

'What do you think he's doing right now?'
'Who?' 'Oh, anyone. I haven't the right
to daydream since I sold it

to my agent.' 'The patient deferral
of the wrath we all deserved,' says Little Dove.
She sharpens her charcoal.

'In his absence story becomes our way
of understanding our own powerlessness
against story. In his story powerlessness

becomes our understanding and our
absence. The hero says, *I am in the way
of the truth and the light*. The hero runs away.'

Generating Relatable Content

At a breakfast meeting Jonah watches his connection –
a middle-man with someone else's hair –
swallow a poached egg in a single gulp.
You know what it's like: you check some food and put your face

directly in the oven's backdraft, momentarily sear your eyes;
the razor in your washbag gives you five
perfect cuts across your fingertip;
a permanent marker permanently marks your shirt.

You resent the world and its implements
for innocently doing what they should.

I don't think he gets me. I pity men who don't.
A well-rounded individual, the operative being *individual*;
whole legends created at whose expense?
I hope you tip your driver handsomely /
it's times like these you miss your family.

He opens wide, a second egg paused on his spoon.
You know the very imports are political,
grain silos, strategic routes, a landscape
designed for car adverts beyond the city walls.
If you are ill at ease you're close to God.

In time a woman comes to sit with them.
He looks at her – thinks gilt-edged books, a puppy, grapes,
the meaning of objects held by saints in icons.

Dinah takes in all of this and smiles. It is
that fast, isn't it? Her knee touches his under the table.

Head of ProphetCon. Familiar with your work.
Are we to assume that before Christ died for our sins
the world was *even worse*?
(You have to stop taking the personal so personally.)
If you can entertain a child you're close to God;
it's how He checks us, every now and then.
We leave a permanent mark on His shirt.

Is he really going to eat *another* egg? He is.

Anxious Lullaby

Who walks out of the sea and smells
of all the merchant's powders?

Here is your bed, my turtledove,
and sixty warriors round it.

'So you see in this beautiful hymn,'
says Little Dove, fluffing the cushions,

'there is the threat of extreme violence
and degradation. Think what they'd do

if they reached the bed: we're the scratch-card,
we're the prize.'

'It is,' agrees Cinnamon Flower,
'a fuckload of warriors.'

'As the turtledoves in the equation
we are to sleep tight,

luxuriate in our downy unconscious,
anticipate nice things tomorrow-ow-ow-ow,

not because it's a wonderful world,
but because we are fortified

[55]

by concentric rings of soldiers.'
Some burly, some surly, some punch their cards early.

We hope the warriors are getting paid enough
We hope their conditions are conducive to their work

We hope the warriors have health insurance
We hope they have a good union to lobby for their rights

We hope none of them goes crazy
We hope a revolution does not foment among the warriors

We hope the supervisors have completed their leadership training
We hope they show no mercy

That's our prayer.
May it please heaven.

The book, like everything else, ends
with the beasts and a question.

And Nobody Was Ever Okay Again

Dinah takes him to a play about childhood.
A seventeen-minute standing ovation.
After one minute Jonah glances around uncomfortably:
cannot quite match the transports of ecstasy.

After the fifth minute he enters a fugue state;
thinks about how weird clapping is.
By the twelfth he is silently weeping,
has never hated more his fellow man.

The tremendous effort it takes
to live even a fairly lousy life.

She links arms with him as they walk by the water's edge.
A ship's bell like a belt buckle clangs.

'Now you're the sort of man
who can't resist the slightest pass at you,
is that correct?'

Jonah finds himself unable to speak;
part of him is still in the audience, applauding.

'I think the story we have to run with here
is your disobedience, your disavowal of the magic,
and yet you're still a prophet. You should keep a diary. I tried

keeping a diary once but it was too painful,' Dinah says.
'Did you know 80% of the time we only use 20% of the words?
Just like 20% of the carpet gets 80% of the wear?
I think I'm falling 80% in love with 20% of you.'

The Internal or Absolute Object

Form

Cosmetics Box asks if they can take
the day off to work on the garden.
Sirocco, jugo, blood rain and abrasions,
intricate devices junked by sediment
in the unmarked form par excellence.
You will garden and, in gardening,
will not garden, thinks Little Dove,
but keeps her counsel; no analogous
counterpart in the receptor language.
Anyway, it's another beautiful day.
'We haven't been out here for ages.'
When I was still in my own country
the infinitive had a substantive function.
Cinnamon Flower unwraps individual
boiled sweets, corpuscle-shaped, lines
them up on the bench. 'Blood, orange
blood, green blood,' she hums. 'What?'
'We were going to trick you and pretend
we thought you could *plant* sweets,'
she explains. 'I said it was a bad idea,'
says Cosmetics Box. 'You're under
a lot of pressure as it is.' 'When
will you plant in your mind what you
have learned,' Little Dove mutters.

Setting

What is that sound from underneath the floorboards?
'In your head.' You don't hear it?
Sounds like muttering. Sometimes a man quietly sobbing.
'That's apposite.' 'Could he be, do you think . . .' 'No.'

While clearing the back forty, Little Dove
finds a coracle and a single oar sealed under a tarp.
Also a wooden chest full of 9-volt batteries.
Hanging on a thick nail, a great coat
with 9-volt batteries sewn into every seam.
Is this his doomsday plan? A battery salesman?
He *was* hitting the gym more than usual.
Decides that she won't tell her sisters, not
because they'd worry but because they wouldn't.

Blue bindweed climbs the wreckage of a wall.
But now we must be about our [*unclear*] business
in a real garden on a real day.
She shakes a tub of white powder
over the turned soil, teeming.
'If the ants saw the poison for what it was
they'd bear the casualties and relocate,
and we'd still have ants. But to them
it appears food. They cannot believe their luck.
They take it into the heart of their nest.'
'It's horrible,' says Cinnamon Flower.
'The growing up and the fading away.'
'That's silly,' says Cosmetics Box,
scratching a welt on her calf. 'Fuck ants.'

Commentary

Six days later an orchard of candy trees
engulfs the house, neat rows, too many,
gold plastic foil budding from the twigs.
Cinnamon Flower starts ordering
automated sprinkler systems. 'Is that ethical?'
'This one is. Here. Honey, that's our old address.'
Narrators define behaviour.
The reason for the clouded glance.
'This should make all of us very angry,'
says Little Dove.
She sits in the double shade
of the awning and the parasol,
with the little clause, asks for death.

A cinch, a narrow belt and your sackcloth
will turn the heaviest heads!

Motive

There is a tiny shift in the meaning,
a tiny shift in the dismal mule's haunches,
tethered to the post with no tether,
no post. 'Go and loose him.'
And if you are carrying a jug of water
pour it on your head.
And if . . . Little Dove is annoyed
by the size of the bagging machine,
the reams of sheet plastic,

the printing press. 'We're going to need
to build a temporary barn or something.'
Cinnamon Flower reclines by the pagoda,
reads *Why Am I Afraid*
To Tell You Who I Am? and swats
away a fly or her concerns.
What portion of your brain can you sublet?

'In my dream,' says Cosmetics Box,
'it was an action movie and I was being pursued
across a city to the municipal water tank by a man
and I started to climb the ladder
and he started to climb the ladder
so I had to climb fast, I could just imagine
his hand closing around my ankle,
so we both climbed fast and at the top,
he must have known – he climbed so fast
so as not to lose me, but he must have known –
when I reached the top of the municipal water tower
I planned to push the ladder away with all my strength
so it would topple right over backwards
and the higher up he was the more
likely he was to be killed by it.
Men must be so conflicted.'

A Man in a City

I

How funny it was to be a man in a city,
hiding his mouth from God, hiding the big pot plant

behind a smaller pot plant. Backpfeifengesicht.
Every meeting was a meal. Get a feel for the place,

they said. Get a feel for the people.
Fill your time with museums for the official version.

Blood-stained tunics, photos of people waiting
for a train they don't know won't contain their loves.

A man sells helium balloons which read
Congrats! On your politics! A busker sings,

*I know a nurse, I know a cop,
my sisters work in agitprop.*

In the city complaining about the city,
Jonah starts to worry he's being used.

A lot of money seems to be changing hands.
He orders a second espresso.

Someone is practising the trumpet with the window open.

2

Refined by two or more days of drunkenness,
dépaysement, a coat that looks stupid.

It takes a while to find an airmail stamp.
He writes a postcard to his daughters:

*I wanted to push you on a swing so when
I passed a swingset in between the blocks I felt sad.*

'I think he thinks we're still children,' says Little Dove.
'Is it worth telling him we're in our 30s,

do you think?' 'I'm not sure he'd take it in.'

3

Open the book at random and apply the passage
to your precise circumstances:

'Show kindness unto the sons of Barzillai
the Gileadite, let them eat at your table.'

4

The pod hotel has 4K screens for walls
so you can choose your backdrop:
volcano, flying buttresses, baked beans.
He takes a meeting in a small black room with a man
who affectionately calls him killer, *Hey, killer.*

5

As for my flock they eat
what you have trodden with your feet.

6

Dinah peels a lychee,
tucks the skin behind a sofa cushion.
We read our own minds constantly. We do.
It's absolutely insane.
Seda vacantis. *A seedy vacation.*

Soft eligibility check,
hard background stairs,
detachment thundering down fast as children
just like they were trained to.
See what you've done, killer?

In heavy rain the people cross the road.
Lavish temples for beloved politicians,

pits of instant death spikes,
pianos in the rain, state orchestras,
their passion etiolated? Let's hope so. No.

He crossed his legs and a document
slid out of the binder.
The man reached for the phone
that fell out of his pocket.
Has someone been stuffing . . .
what is this, *lychee* skin?

7

Dinah sits pretzeled in the Romanesque arcade.
A cat attacks a strip of skin cast out of a stall.
'It's fine, to be clear, if you want to see other people.'
There are crimes against humanity
then there's being *liked*, you know?

Senseless Ornaments

. . . it might be altogether more accurate to say that the Times of Day
were an afterthought. [. . .] Not until actually doing it did
Michelangelo know precisely what it was he meant to do.
         — Gunther Neufeld on Michelangelo's 'Il Giorno e La Notte'

Regarding her bored sisters,
art history seems as good a discipline as any.
'If you can access the innermost temple of your mind . . .'
Cinnamon Flower snorts.
Cosmetics Box unwraps a disposable vape.

'We are become more verb than noun.'
You can see it.
Without altogether renouncing your wits
you can see it.

When the whole family wants to learn always
everyday that is always fun and energizing!

You laugh at the world's LinkedIn bromides
until it's time to raise a child
and then you love too much.

'I don't know what I'm supposed to think or feel
when I look at something.'
'When you look at art?'

'*At anything!*' says Cosmetics Box.
She blows a plume of crystal mist.
'Well that's a good foundation.'

'Days of footage but no sense to be made of any of it,'
Cinnamon Flower protests.
Her ribbons are a strip of celluloid.
'What possible good will this do
for us or anyone else?'

'It will, I think, be understood
that the attempt to meet that question
cannot hope to offer more than a fragmentary answer,'
says Little Dove.

The night has life because it sleeps:
try to wake the sculpture,
the sculpture will not wake, but
that is not to say it won't wake up next time.

'My boyfriend says he can make statues laugh,'
says Cinnamon Flower.
'Dump him, girl,' says Little Dove.
'And bronze serpents writhe.'
'That's just art-shaming by another name,'
says Little Dove. 'Each age dreads its automata.'
'I don't know what you mean.'
'Plus he's old.' Plus he's possessed by

day's choleric temper,
pain, contempt or revenge.
Day faces away, twists back its head to look at us.
Right arm stretches behind as if to fetch something – what?
A camera? A bowl of grapes? A book? A crossbow?
Just stay right where you are a sec, don't move . . .
'Perhaps all four combined into a charm.'
Only Day's forearm is sculpted.
The Day has life because it is unfinished.

A Wake

I don't think I can do this anymore.
What.
I don't want to do the work.
But —
I want to be drinking afterwards already. In celebration of the work.
I don't —
Now. One way of cutting straight to that moment, one way of
    circumnavigating all the work, it seems to me, is to be drunk.
    That's the way I see it.
What do you really want?
I cannot stress this enough: I want to be drunk. I want either to be
    drunk or *building up to* being drunk again.
I see.
That is the only thing: the building up, the fortification of my
    body and mind by whatever means at hand so that I may
    commence drinking again — potions, complex carbohydrates,
    affirmations — it may at times, it may, some days, be difficult,
    but I am up to that.
To what?
To that complexity. I don't care what it does to me.
Hmm.
You will say, In that case, sir, you are living in a wake.
You are.
A wake? I'll say. A wake, you'll nod.
I do say that. A wake. Not a celebration, but a wake.
My own? I'll say. My own?! (I will, at this point, be quite cross
    with you.) No, everyone's, you'll say.
No, everyone's wake — I do say that. I'm saying it now. A wake.

Third Book of Maccabees

I

'The papers say we're going to need 500 elephants
and we're going to need to get them injured and harassed, so they
   attack.'

Cinnamon Flower looks up from her stack of newspapers.
'I thought those were for the puppy,' says Little Dove.

'And by *we* they don't mean *us*,' says Cinnamon Flower.
'What are you going to do –
are you going to renounce your faith?
Feels a little rich to avoid being crushed by your own house
only to be crushed by 500 drunken elephants in a theatre.'

'No good ever comes of animals drinking,'
says Cosmetics Box. 'Imagine if the puppy got drunk –
it would be horrible.'

'He'll oversleep and then forget what he was angry about,'
says Little Dove. 'That's Ptolemy. Then the elephants
will turn on him, he'll honour us with feasts
and we'll petition him to execute anyone
who renounced their faith. So watch yourselves.'

2

. . . and when he was slowly dissolving
in the belly of the beast
you returned him unharmed to his family
oh please oh may it please you
the whole crowd of children
and their parents supplicate you with tears
we know you like that . . .

3

Or do you?
Little Dove receives a vision:
A year has passed.
Jonah has not spoken a word since his return.
A permanent shade has fallen on him.
She bathes her father's forehead,
her sisters lean together in the awning,
upright basses, detuned, gravitating,
as we do, towards an all-controlling author.
Failing that, each other.
'You need to find some little things
to take pleasure in,' she'll tell them.
'A good cup of coffee,
the idea of the secure self.'
I know, she'll bathe and bathe
her father's forehead, *you have been forced
into a position of self-negation
from which death is the only escape.*
Each night she'll hold a cowrie shell —
decorated with exactly this scene —
to his ear until he falls asleep.

Here He Risks His Honour

As far as Dinah is concerned, God
will use a prophet's natural proclivities,
therefore he is duty bound to indulge them.
Vanity, obsession with sex, boredom,
drunkenness, despair. 'Lust for power?'
No, not that one. 'Well, we're all missing something.'

What were you trying to convince us of again?'
An absolute and totalising cruelty.
'Oh, yes, that. Must take a toll.'
They exchange a pallbearer's glance.

You want to get a little out of your head, always.

All of this, you know, could be happening inside your body.
Which if it is a temple might as well include the street,
and if that, then the surrounding commercial and residential
    district too,
and if that, why not the whole area code,
why not the city, the country, the continent?

'Thus spake the fat astronaut.'

Dinah, please.

Does alcohol exist within the body anyway? he googles.
Yes, many marketplaces and manufacturers.

'And what of someone else's body?' she says.
'I think I know just the thing to buoy you up.'

A little lunch, a little death.

Having sensed a vague spiritual presence
we've upgraded your flight. Take your place
with the favoured.

He wakes up in the same hotel room, flicks through
the potential views: stormy meadow, outer darkness.
Pores over his pour-over. A message fills the screen:
Come back to mine, I miss you.

'There was a time when you simply didn't have anything to say:
you cared only for your fluffy neon pencil case,
the eyes you'd glued to him, a part of you stayed inside him
when you zipped him up. But now, because of that,
you want to be everyone's boyfriend:
a consoling hand on the small of the back,
impulsive slamming kiss in a dark doorway,
a whisper: no one understands you like I do;
I see the way you look at her, and her, and her;
disgusting how you spread your love so thin,
and flavourless. I'm not even angry.'

Yes, yes, he says, All of that is true. What of it?

Dinah does something to the dulcimer. 'Shall we go out
for a drink?' He leans off the side of the bed,
tries to separate his clothes from hers. Sharps, flats,
you don't know anything beyond that. 'What I'm saying is
you overlook the work that made you the perfect vessel.'

They both look out the window at the same time
and see his new girlfriend waiting to cross the street,
a neutral expression on her face, holding a large box.
'You'll have nothing but grief with that one,' she says.

The cocktail bar has so many potted plants
he feels like an animal in its natural habitat
wondering whether to trust the hand of man.

'You said some awful things to me last night.'
I say some awful things to everyone.
'What would your daughters think?'
She smiles into her Old Fashioned, takes a sip.

They would think, When you divert a river
it presents a consistent set of physical
and ecological challenges.

An Inconsiderable Village

Little Dove surveys the men who dig the wine press.
'Do you need any help?' They swing their axes
into the hard earth. One wipes his brow

with a dark red rag. 'Excuse me?' she says.
'Fine then.' It is never clear to her whether
she is being ignored or doesn't exist.

Amittai doesn't recognise her, or Cinnamon Flower
or Cosmetics Box, but then he's mad;
it's not a level plane. But where is she supposed to find

true north? 'They'll take our money, sure enough,'
says Cinnamon Flower, transferring meal to a jar.
The town itself, *die ubersetzer, enstellt,*

made fictional by one typo in Joshua; you send
a messenger down the synapses, down the words,
the digging of the wine press, the cow of the guitars,

several guitars leaning against a single cow,
false friends in the servant's quarters,
crocodiles reflected in a disco ball. It's maybe

the one mistake that saved them, escaping
from the frieze to the brocade. 'So we should
at least make an effort to look nice.' Oh come on.

'We were in our brother's house,' she says.
'We had so much wine and snacks, we were
so happy.' Stop staring at the wall like that.

There must be *some* advantage in not having
a speaking part. Something happened back there
and I only am escaped alone to tell thee.

Écrivains Sans Frontières

The last five minutes have been in colour,
      sails on the horizon, horses in the rain:
both kinds of thinking. All two. Chess tables
      to take your mind off it. If the world hates you . . .
A pretty boy with small eyes stares at him.

I find the coffee here a little strong, don't you?
      Who sent you? Dinah?
Who? No, I'm here for work. I'm here five days.
      The boy is a writer on a diplomatic assignment.
And what does that involve?

I tell them what it's like being a writer.
      Do they like that? Do they like you?
They fawn over me and sometimes tell me off.
      My role, as I see it, is a benign form of art-washing.
We want you to know we recognise you,

acknowledge your sovereignty. Here's a basket of figs,
      a bolt of silk, one of our minor poets.
They pay you? *Handsomely. I'm getting more*
      for this than for my last three books combined.
He drains his tiny cup down to the silt.

You know, I've been all over. Secular and holy temples,
  washed an elephant with my tears,
smiled or bowed to envoys as was fitting,
  I've eaten the braised anus of a hog.
In one city I couldn't get a drink.

That was hard. And it occurred to me
  that God is showing me the world before He ends it!
Why you? *Why me! Indeed!*
  He has a little pin-badge of a book.
Where are you from? *I'm sorry?*

What nationality. *Oh. I don't really*
  go in for that sort of thing anymore.
English. He pauses. Once, perhaps.
  You can't just . . . I met an oracle
three days ago. I sat with him four hours in the sand.

He told me that in my past life I was a river.
  Which river? Where?
Ah, I see, he says. *Like that, is it?*
  A storm reveals the move you could've made.
It is, says Jonah, yes, I am like that, it is.

Calvus Benedictio

'When we say pseudo-Joachim, what does it mean?'
'We've never been sure,' says Cinnamon Flower.
'We've lost the knack of reading long-form prose,'
says Cosmetics Box. 'It means sufficient things
were misattributed to the real Joachim that we lack
any other way to designate,' says Little Dove.
'This creates a new person.' 'That's all it takes?'
says Cinnamon Flower. Tying back her hair
she pauses to scratch an ant bite on her ankle.
On worn-out chairs, in evening wear,
in the waning turmeric light they look as plain or
beautiful as you would like to imagine them.

Understanding the Historical Person

*The exact meaning of Tathāgata is unknown, but it is often thought
to mean either 'one who has thus gone' (tathā-gata), 'one who has
thus come' (tathā-āgata), or even 'one who has thus not gone' (tathā-
agata). This is interpreted as signifying that the Tathāgata is beyond
all coming and going – beyond all transitory phenomena.*

Jonah next sees the writer in the market.
    Against a backdrop of dusty watermelons
he smokes a short cigarette
    from a little gold box,

haggles inexpertly over a bronze elephant.
    Aha, he says, looks up, *my father figure.*
Looking for a place to preach? Not here.
    Already saved or beyond redemption? Ha.

It is no business of mine.
    Not keen on the humidity, but . . .
the drowsy bugs are easier to swat.
    I'm reading at the embassy tonight –

maybe you'd like a ticket? Free wine. No.
    I find I get less hungry in the heat, don't you?
I must remind myself to eat for fuel.
    You'll join me for a drink perhaps? I can't.

I'm really rather lonely here, you see;
        I have no Sancho Panza, Bosworth, Damis.
Sometimes I cry in rainy parks or on
        the immaculate underground, or on

escalators in 20-storey shopping malls,
        I don't look back, I cast no glance over
my shoulder in case I turn to salt.
        Brass bowls for tributes,

flower of the almond tree,
        offerings of syrup, little coins, blood.
I thought about what you said. You did? I did.
        'I cannot be from my country for I have no stake in it.'

Was my conclusion.
        But if you had your little house, you'd fly your flag?
Only if it came under attack. Besides
        don't we all have a common enemy

whoever or wherever we may be?
        Who makes our modest dreams unreachable?
Our only choice: augmenting our credulity
        about their good intentions, either way,

make no mistake:
      they'd rent us our own faces if they could.
Who's of their ranks? Not I.
      But you'd like to be?

If I came back as a tiger, like Siddhartha,
      I'd voluntarily starve myself to death,
he says, and gets a distant look.
      Well, okay. *Tell me, what would you prophesy to me?*

Bad things are coming.
      Now now; that's cheating, isn't it? Bad things.
You may find yourself possessed of a heroism
      you didn't know you had, or you may scream

and push a child in front of you,
      who knows? *Who knows. I'd like to think –*
One thing you're right withal:
      none of this is really about you anymore.

Festschrift

'Fettschrift' is a feminine noun. Remember that.
It means boldface.

A 'festschrift' is a celebration of an academic's life
with contributions from peers and well-wishers.

'Jonah literally means *dove*,' says Cosmetics Box,
looking up from her book. 'So

it's all very well for you.' 'I'm not saying,'
says Little Dove, 'that this is easy.'

My heart's a fragile concertina
your hardy squeezebox wouldn't know.

'What will be in our father's festchrift, do you think?
The courtiers resented him of course,

whether his prophecies came true or not.
We'll have to round up some people who liked him

for hating the same things they did.' She sighs.
'He's coming back, you know,' says Cinnamon Flower.

'He never left,' Cosmetics Box insists, and stamps, which makes
a book fall off the shelf and land spreadeagled

on the centrefold: *Arguments in Favour*
of the Economic Reform of Paradise; Icons of purgatory,

a bearded anti-saint who shrugs and mouths stop painting me.
A pornographic playing card

as bookmark falls between the floorboards.
The difference between a rebel and a revolutionary.

Though I Fear Not God, Nor Regard Man

Jonah chews tobacco, visits the arcades
    of the necropolis. Someone else's dead.
Finds the writer with his well-chewed pencil out.
    The graveyard is a graveyard for the idea of a graveyard;

There's just too many of us now for such luxury.
    Finding some inspiration in the field?
You think that's why I'm here? Can you imagine?
    'What I did on my holiday.' Now really,

you must think more of me than that. A dog,
    the imagination asks for darker meats than these
and duller, too: shed-meats, the meat of scrublands,
    double yellow lines. A man with a plastic bag.

Feed it too much and it gets fat and dies.
    A blue-black butterfly lands upon his head.
Like every mind, it matters – No, fuck off,
    he tells the boy who tries to shine his shoes.

It must get tiresome, being passed around,
    a meagre bauble polished like a coin.
I might ask you the same question, you know?
    What are you doing here mooching around

so far from where you've been required to go?
      A jackal whines, deep in the hyacinth.
The writer tosses him a gravy bone.
      I'm only stopping here a week or two,

then further West. As far as I can get.
      Well careful, or you'll make it all the way around,
ha ha ha ha. I'll take that as advised.
      Too hot for levity, so Jonah turns on him.

If your country was instantly wiped off the face of the earth
      would anybody even notice?
The writer shrugs. *You could say that*
      about any country really, couldn't you?

You once ransacked the world! He shrugs again.
      'It serves our humility to have so evil been.'
Who's that? *Myself. It's from a poem called*
      'To Weigh a Planet, What Would be the Scales?'

What dreamlike fabrication of the weights,
      and where to build your welded conglomeration
of asteroids, space junk and meteors?
      You'll get your answer but it will no longer apply

to the new world you've brought into being.
      That's the problem, isn't it, I think?
Open your heart. Now close it again. There.
      Dust settles before the crash this time;

the lesson is it always *has* been out of joint.
      Like scenes excised for blasphemy or brevity –
Messiah trampled in a modern city street –
      the drunkard brings his vomit, the poet his song.

Nevertheless, there is no excuse for bad art.
      Later on a black and white TV
stuck fizzing in the corner of his room,
      a towel around his waist, he sees

the item on the local news: *Ten people*
      kidnapped including one British national,
a writer, though on reflection, truth be told,
      he hadn't really written anything of note.

CHAPTER III

In which Jonah, fleeing a conflict he wants no part in,
is swallowed by a great fish, transported many miles,
then is vomited up on the shores of Nineveh and
delivers his prophecy.

Lecture 3: No Arts; No Letters; No Society

That Jonah is swallowed by a great fish is the easiest way to introduce his story to anyone – oh yeah, that guy. An act of God too ridiculous to be heavy handed. My hand is light, come learn of me. There are many variations and by laying one on top of the other like warped transparencies we may begin to get a complete picture.

Ψ

In one version the Lord 'set out' a great fish; 'appointed' a great fish; 'arranged for' a great fish; 'provided' a great fish; now the Lord 'had prepared' a great fish; 'designated' a great fish; 'destined' a great fish; 'sent' a great fish; only once 'commanded' a great fish.

Ψ

In the next version Jonah is swallowed by a great fish which contains an exact replica of the world. Here the narrative continues and he is spat up in Nineveh, but it is a Nineveh within the false world of the great fish, where he lives out the rest of his days, a hero absent from the real, a boardgame piece, a laughing cow cheese earring depicting a laughing cow.

Ψ

In the next version the Great fish has a name, Leviathan, from Psalm 103. *There go the great ships and there is that Leviathan whom Thou hast made to take his sport therein.* Wherein 'that' Leviathan does

[93]

not indicate one example of a Leviathan but a genial familiarity
with the one and only Leviathan.

Ψ

In the next version, part of the Midrash Cinematic Universe, the
great fish is a rival to Leviathan; he fears Leviathan and knows for a
fact that Leviathan plans to swallow him, and his passenger, whole.
In this version Jonah must steer the great fish like a submarine,
to actively pursue Leviathan, against the great fish's better judge-
ment. And when they round on him, Jonah must show Leviathan
his circumcised penis as a sign that he is favoured by God, at which
Leviathan will take fright and swim away. Oscar-bait. It is bad
form to fail to acknowledge the author of the original novel *and* the
translator. 'Frivolous and puerile' – Calvin on the Midrash, cf. the
total anathema on Calvinism, but if you're raised in a tributary you
rarely acknowledge the river. At the end of time, Jonah will return
to the ocean, capture Leviathan with ropes and bring him up to
Paradise where he'll be sliced up alive and fried in ginger, garlic,
soy and served to the elect.

Ψ

In the next version Jonah is swallowed by a naturalistic great fish.
Inside the great fish's stomach it is very pink, very dark, and he
can barely move. It feels squishy, but tight as a last embrace. After
three days the great fish is caught in a vast net by a fishing trawler,
hauled aboard by seven men gripping the net like climbers. The
great fish is sliced open and Jonah, along with many smaller fish,
squid with shells half cracked, tiny creeping things and scuttling

crabs, spills out onto the deck to the astonishment of the hard-to-ruffle crew. He takes a ragged breath and cries out *Agggggh!* His great beard and his long hair have been burned off by gastric acids, which is why he is often depicted emerging bald in art. Once he has been spoon fed enough tomato and fish stew, nursed back to health in scratchy, hessian linen, Jonah asks the fishermen where they are going, where they mean to sell their cargo, where their week's work ends, and they say *Nineveh* and he says –

Ψ

In the next version the great fish is an erotic novel, a perfect insertion, carnal fantasies that assail one in the night, great fish as patron of those who are utterly lost to the pursuit of physical pleasure, who find themselves able to think of little else.

Ψ

In the next version Jonah made the whole thing up, but nobody can say for sure. Nobody can prove or disprove his version of events. Jonah has washed up in Nineveh and he seems to be having a good time even though he protests that he wishes he was literally anywhere else, claims that he was swallowed and transported there by a great fish. Right. Seems like something someone who *hadn't* been swallowed and transported by a great fish would say. Jonah either believes his own story or he doesn't; a passionately guarded delusion or a ruse. If the former, the skin around his eyes tightens and cracks as he insists, his beard grows wild, he corners you at a wedding.

Ψ

In the next version Jonah is a Christian videogame soundtracked by a Christian rock band. It's odd because you're a hero but your quest involves literally robbing graves, or murdering angels with an enchanted golden double-headed axe, or failing to put aside the cares of this life. The great fish is asleep and everything that happens in the narrative is within the dream of the great fish, and Jonah's quest is to wake him up, and when he wakes the great fish up the dream will end, regardless of the emotional bonds Jonah has built with the people he's met in the city, all of whom will immediately cease to exist. And you can tell, in retrospect, that it was a dream because some of the characters belonged to other franchises.

Ψ

In the next version the great fish represents a proscenium arch, the act of opening a giant book, and Jonah enters a story about his own life in which a great fish swallows him.

The Elders Gather

For St Methodius the great fish represents *time*, the three days and nights in its belly correspond to past, future, and present. The pure spiritual substance, the three days' entombment, the parallels between this and Christ's three days in the belly of Hades.

St Cyril of Jerusalem says Christ and Jonah were both sent to preach repentance; Jonah is thrown in like a soluble aspirin whereas Christ rebukes the storms and the sea.

St John Chrysostom gives direct voice to Christ, Jonah is the servant but I am the master. Coming not to threaten or demand an account but to pardon. Jonah runs away for fear of ridicule, but Christ embraces mockery.

St Gregory the Theologian refers repeatedly to his own unnamed instructor and assigns many of his insights to this teacher rather than taking credit for them himself. He refers to Jonah's 'stolen self'. Jonah knew very well he couldn't really hide from God, but resented so thoroughly the passing over of the grace of prophecy to the Gentiles he thought he'd try anyway. In repentance we are aware that we're probably going to do it again, but we are wrong to feel this way; right now we are repenting; right now is all we have and for God the indivisible moment is not so much an hour, a week, an aeon but an individual eternity among eternities . . .

For St Ambrose, Christ is the true Jonah, who took captivity captive, stayed three days in the belly of the earth. He mentions Job, who mentions sea monsters.

In certain Rabbinical dialogues the King of Nineveh is Pharaoh, the lone survivor of the parting of the Red Sea, the only Egyptian who didn't drown, was kept alive as a witness and, after some time, founded the city of Nineveh (an advanced city with canals and running water). Hence he knew the power of the acts of God and Jonah knew he knew; the dates are very much disputed here.

St Ambrose says Jonah is *a type of saviour*, traces his lineage to the book of Kings and thus does away with the Book of Jonah as a parody. The judgements of the Lord are a great abyss, we cannot know them.

In all their words they sigh and close their ledgers, they drain their cups of water, they slowly turn to look you in the eye.

First Prayer

Verse-by-verse anagram of Jonah 2: 2–10

Moldiest altruism factory.
Addled homeowners threaten our stormy hellhole.
Be off! Edict (i): ah comedy, *oui*, very.
Deepening foul-mouth:
aesthete, faith, heron.
Yet an armoured entrance, unmatched.

A sad lawbreaker nervously overrated memes.
And I thought: Hobbes affirmed Rome,
yes, you, re. your woke litigation lily,
your hope moltenly up-tempo,
yr tableware a cheated knot.
Adherence moped mute; bounded homeward, unswayed.

Take a window minute . . .

Honest footnotes on absurd doctors,
athlete-ghostwritten, LMAO.
Beg Thor, buyout fervour (either plummy tipoff,
weight of my dog drool).

Your lyrical appendectomy, a lurid mother.
Admin feinted with hookup theory.

(*sotto*) Abysmal ferret, emote hollowly.

Rothko-youth employee.
You chose sultry vapor in a firmware watermill.
And I, with a knavish cognitive fog,
facetiously meteoric.

Me, what I adeptly wove:
chortles reissued,
choruses relisted,
hostelries cursed,
rescue is the Lord's.

Plainsong

Improvisation on Jonah 2:2-10

I cried out from my luxury condominium
    to the Lord, and He answered me.
From the commonly-owned area I called out –
    Oh Lord hear my voice albeit my mouth
is full of sashimi, this is the equivalent
    of something better, it was ever thus.
Flight failed me and I lay desperate, whatever I want.
    I'm like one of those naked human trays
but instead of lying meekly on a long table
    surrounded by depressed businessmen
twitching their chopsticks, I'm in a hearse
    in a glass case in a museum and I ruined it
because I won't stop talking.
    You threw me into the depths of a vast dining hall
Everyone said it's so nice to see you in a dinner jacket
    and I thought:
Why did nobody advise me against that lapel pin?
    My forehead was decanting sweat,
my bow-tie hadn't been fastened properly,
    hands tore at me and tried to pet me,
one man I had to murder because he kept interrupting;
    a shame because he'd been fully analysed.
I felt so transfigured and boring and kept saying I was sorry,
    all Your breakers and waves collapsed upon me;
the weeds were wrapped about my head and I said,
    I am cast out of your sight, Lord, but once again

I will look on that alleyway and emote,
        but once again I will hear Your voice.
You gave me a car and a sense of self-worth and
        after what happened last time
I'm surprised anyone is still returning my calls.
        I got home in exactly one piece.
I took a carton of eggs to the retired soprano,
        she threw the eggs from her 12th floor window
at every bearded man who passed
        and used the carton to store trinkets,
but one of them wouldn't fit so she gave it to me.
        It's so nice, after a party, to just *not be at a party*,
even if that suggests some tectonic problem.
        Oh Lord pardon my iniquities, my sins rise above me
like a tower made of sores on the cover of a death metal album
        every note mourns my birth and celebrates my death;
I cannot discern a metric principle,
        maybe it was translated. How manifold are Your works
Oh Lord, but we added too many extra folds
        now we can fold ourselves away and keep folding
and mistake it for real life.

Between Mouthfuls

Treated text, Jonah 2:2–10

I called out from –
To the –
From the –
You –
You –
And the –
All your –
Streamed –
And I thought –
I am –
Yet again –
On –
Water –
The –
Weed –
To the –
The –
But you –
O –
As my –
The –
And –
To your –
Those who –
Will –

And I –
Let me –
What I –
Rescue –

Serious Women

The telephone within the great fish rings.

'Bibliomancy, divination, seances,' says Dinah.

I'm good, he tells her. Things okay with you?

A memory game. Turn over one card.
Then another.

I miss you, by the way. I forgot
to tell you anything about myself.

'No, that's okay. That's *my* job,' she says.

I'm sorry. Serious women make me incredibly silly.

'What does that say about you?'

That I'm eager to oblige.

'Do serious men have the same effect?'

I've never met one.

I'm not in a very good place right now.

I used to think it was funny . . .

I used to love you. I still do, but I used to.

Little Dove Considers Pulling Up
the Floorboards

Cosmetics Box swipes through logos
on her tablet. 'Bad. Stupid. Fussy.
Clearly AI. Where do you find a good
graphic designer these days?'

'They're the new bohemians,' says
Little Dove and goes back to
Miss Macintosh, My Darling.
The buyers have fallen through,

the house is always flooding
and creeps ever closer to the cliff.
'It's so funny,' says Cinnamon Flower,
'that you read all of those books

where absolutely everyone is dead.
I mean it's true isn't it?' she appeals
to her other sister. 'They *are*, right?'
'Dead,' agrees Cosmetics Box.

'Whatever they did, whatever they
thought or said or felt, they're dead.'
Little Dove is about to lecture them
on the eternal present, and Boethius,

who is also dead, and somehow
this makes everyone else feel
twice as dead, which strikes her
as so ineluctably sad that she stifles

a sob. Her pen pal – a *writer*, from
England, hasn't replied to her last letter
and he's normally so punctual.
'I heard it again,' says Cinnamon Flower,

and pounces on the floor. 'I swear it's him.'
'Right,' says Little Dove. Her novel
hits her ankle like an anvil. She goes
to fetch her crowbar from the shed.

Dans le Gros Poisson

He's been in here for forty hours
      invoking all the heavenly powers,
but nothing doing.
      The ghosts of other nation's
flags strung between the gory bowers.
      Given a skylight
he could divine upon a star
      called Epsilon Lyrae
or Double Double,
      or polish his Deserter's Cross,
or watch the men debate the toss,
      or take the trouble to arrange a séance,
read the entrails of a whale
      within a whale,
or call himself from his own phone,
      pay back a loan with other loans;
agnostic agonistes moans
      beneath the rubble.
Your friends are pre-political;
      it's hard to find convincing words
or justify your favoured slurs,
      but if you'd read the books and if you knew
who'd written them, I mean,
      an air-strike on a festival
of neutral bubbles.

Don't waste your breath on cover versions,
or watering the grey nasturtiums;
    the prophet, God's blank Scrabble tile
spells something odder . . .
    (Their minds are bursting at the seams
with cross-stitched sentimental memes –
    they're easy fodder.)
See that you're ready to receive it,
    see the fruit on the vine and leave it,
forget your station;
    most of us lack the ways or means
to write something on Benzedrines
    or inspiration.
Hard not to throw onto the fire
    my obsolete propaganda
(or find a buyer).

Poem Beginning with the Line
'My Thoughts are Childlike in Their Simplicity'

My thoughts are childlike in their simplicity;
I'm either frightened or so happy I could die –
I either race across the station to your arms
or I accidentally broke your window
and I'm trying to hide by screwing up my eyes;
and yet the years flick by like frantic shrimp
to me; a century doesn't seem very long at all –
the dates in parenthesis after an author's name;
the mummified cat, a little wadded bowling pin,
its face drawn on with stitches, natural dyes,
still looks just fine after 2,400 years;
transported from museum to museum
in its strongbox, in its armoured motorcade,
the little mummified cat, for seventeen and a half
million dollars, going once, going twice . . .

Jonah is Vomited Up on the Shore of Nineveh

In a pixel-rot ecru hotel room
Jonah decides to come clean.
On a Zoom call, in a towel gown,
in the formidable morning.
The promenade where he will
deliver his prophecy visible
from the window. Someone
selling shellfish from a crate.
You can be nice to your waiter
and still be reprehensible, that's
the intentional fallacy, but
the reverse doesn't hold. Oh
it's a petit bourgeois Tuesday
for the petit bourgeoisie.

A functionary visits with a picture
from his daughters: a colour-
pencil drawing of a sea monster
decorated with glitter shells.
I don't think this is them.
She scowls. *That took me hours.*

The operation was a complete success,
she says. Oh yes?
*Yes. We swapped around your brain
and your heart. How do you feel?*

What do I *think*, you mean.

I think I am a living rebuke.
Is that why I'm still alive?
Woah. Woah as in stop or woah
as in you just blew my mind?

Do you have a product, aside from
the spittle-flecked roar of the Almighty?
He's not like that. *What is he like?*
He's like grief. *Okay*, she says.
We can use that.

Expolitio / Exergasia

Jonah accepts an invitation to a balcony.
A cultural retreat where freethinkers gather
for a holiday to share their views, unruffled
by . . . unencumbered by the . . . without fear of . . .
It is hard to know exactly what they mean
by 'freethinking'. They call themselves The New
something or other. But soon it's clear
they're preening idiots, nursing perceived slights
over bottles without labels in mental gardens
so untended. One might say 'damaged'
were one feeling generous and were
there a mind worth ruining between them.
A little harsh there, buddy. What? Are you
going to throw me overboard again?
He'd fall fifteen feet to the yellow grass,
maybe break an elbow or a leg. I'm not sure
what you mean by cancellation – I think
you mean that people should be forced
to still engage with your work. That's really funny.
A pet tapir curls its nose into an open binbag.
Admonished, it slopes off. *My thoughts will not
cater to duke or dictator.* A little damp smoke
rises from the mushroom barbecue. It's what
society usually allows a symbol to be.
Many people in the afterlife are convinced
it's just a dream. If you're trying to convert me
to the cult of myself, try harder. I'd say

the bar is pretty goddamn low. I may not
be wise but I'm very good at making fun of
other people who are also not wise. A man,
by contrast, is just a worm for hedonism.
I just want to be considered the best
at talking about what it's like to be alive;
I don't see why being a terrible person
should have any bearing on that whatsoever.

After lunch there is a trip to a local crevasse
from which a visible miasma emanates:
off-green phosphines, isocyanides, acetone.
Some fall in, some hang out by the minivan.
Jonah leans over the ravine, inhales
and shuts his eyes. No more ridiculous
than any other group, all told: poacher
recognises poacher. But be careful
what you sacrifice is yours to sacrifice.

Do You Still Get Nervous?

Backstage, Jonah is fitted with a contact microphone. A pep talk. A commercial publisher faces many infrastructural burdens, but in this case *YOU* are the method, both of storing prophecy and its distribution. We've heard a lot about you and have been looking forward to experiencing you for ourselves. We have already sold 250% of the shares in your prophecy, losses which will be easily recouped as long as you don't – I mean to say as long as this goes well, which I'm sure it will. PRs have no more idea of how to talk to an artist than a wild yak.

The lights temporarily dazzle him. He is surprised by the reverb on his voice. After five minutes he knows that he's completely lost the room – there's a look that sets in like time-lapse mould. You realise that you have based your entire sense of self on something shaky and unreliable – the passing approval of others; what drives the false prophet and if they are any different; confused ideas of the vulgar on the subject . . . What is interesting is not your prophecy but your refusal.

There's an old Soviet joke about Stalin going undercover to a cinema; during the newsreel Stalin appears on screen and the audience stand, applaud and cheer. Stalin, in disguise, remains seated, taking it in. The man next to him bends down to whisper in his ear, *None of us want to do this either, comrade, but please, it would be safer if you stood.*

Flat White (A Prophecy)

It is good for people to have a seat at the table, but it is still a table. A table in a stately home with lion's paws, a glass table in a silver boardroom.

Everyone should have some shade in the shady cabal.

In the future shade will be sold at £5 for fifteen minutes. In the great deserts pocked with salt deposits. We will rent a little cardboard shield for £20 an hour and lie with our heads in its shade, murmuring, *Oh god I feel so much better*. You are currently on the run because you got angry and tore the cardboard shield into shreds when it was time to give it back. This is the attention economy.

Φ

There was a man who subscribed to everything. For a small monthly fee he was a member of every theatre and art gallery so that he was given access to a special room and a free small glass of wine as well as advanced tickets at a modest reduction; a sponsor of every podcast, YouTube channel, web comic and publisher he enjoyed, and he enjoyed many and felt that he ought not to receive their labours for nothing. A prolific benefactor who received over 900 emails from his various clients and sponsees each day and had to spend certain of his off hours sorting through them. These were tiny, Lilliputian arrows with ropes attached and within a year he was bankrupt and in tens of thousands of pounds of debt.

Some felt that he had undertaken his own ruination as a kind of immersive piece of performance art, that what he had sculpted, out of time, out of his life and his own body, contained a message or a comment that we might heed or respond to.

Some felt that there ought to be a GoFundMe to bail him out, a GoFundMe to the like of which the man himself might have contributed were he not now insolvent. That if he was guilty of largesse and generosity beyond his means – beyond any realistic means – who among us could not imagine going the same way if we took – at face value and that only – every request we received. No, he was a martyr, a martyr of the arts, and had perished for a better cause, a greater world.

Some felt that he was an imbecile and deserved all that had happened to him and worse.

Some seemed to recall a later newspaper article wherein it was reported that he was starting to get back on his feet, as they say, had found a workable debt consolidation payment plan and a middle management role in life-insurance and that he was finding pleasure in small things, like sitting on a bench and looking at sycamore seeds pirouetting into the basketball court, reflecting that, after all, there were still pleasures, there were still small things.

In whichever case he is no use to any of us now.

Φ

Something holds my tongue, the fear of sentimentality, which if you should avoid in writing you should absolutely avoid in real life. It is not gentleness, it is not kind. Sentimentality is simply *not listening to anyone*. A failure to adapt in response to stimuli. A plant would do better.

The idea that there might emerge a writer so brilliant and compelling and − whatever, new superlatives would have to be coined − that their work immediately reverses the systematic, multilayered, compound damage of the long 1990s and the decades hence. We might wall ourselves up in a cave and wait for them. Probably I am hypersensitive to this denial of basic civility . . .

Φ

What we ask of children is completely ridiculous. What is there to say?

There's something off about me. I say the wrong things. My attempts at being funny embarrass my contemporaries. I am attacked, with good reason, like the weak hunter who slows down the pack.

Actually many ancient tribes demonstrated great thought-fulness and kindness to their weaker members.

What are *we* hunting?

Some distant relative in the golden age of journalism worked as a theatre critic despite little to no enthusiasm for theatre − that was how it was back then and such was the insatiable demand for the written word that you needed neither to like nor have any particular expertise in your area of expertise − as long as you were the right kind of chap you need have no passion for your passions nor conviction in your convictions. He would sit in the theatre bar drinking and base his copy on what he overheard other people saying in the interval.

Φ

I could never marry a surgeon, they have absolutely no regard for human life. I like it when you're not sure where the joke is.

As in interpretations of attention in the brain, attention in artificial systems is helpful as a way to flexibly wield limited resources. At some point an artificial bottleneck must be introduced. This is called a context vector.

Φ

There must be some tone which is neither priest nor politician nor comedian on a panel show nor national treasure nor brash upstart nor nod to the gallery nor gurn to the court nor flowers to the disappointed nor wink to the camera nor scampers unobtrusively like a ball boy to retrieve nor suspect guru nor fault nor double fault nor last summation nor opening gambit nor victim impact statement nor sermon on the mount nor tilted head of the obliging nor dissembling boyfriend nor snarling of the cornered rat nor absolute centre of the self, but if there is I'm yet to find it.

Φ

In modernity childhood and old age became distinct realms, to be left and to be entered, as if there were some kind of neutral zone within the human lifespan. Good health and illness, the private and the public, work and leisure, wealth and poverty, the inner and the outer life.

Φ

Tired of such secular pieties.

The milk foam of excess individualism. This phenomenon which appears even in times of greater prosperity.

Ending a poem on a resonant well-crafted image is an act of spiritual violence.

[119]

CHAPTER IV

In which Jonah's prophecy is met with instant repentance,
unnatural enthusiasm, flattery and imitation. Jonah does
not like this and hopes the city still might be destroyed.
Nevertheless it is unsafe for him to return home.
God decides to talk to him again.

Lecture 4: The Totally Wrong Stories to Live By

One hundred pages of throat clearing. Cited in Sherwood, p. 107, Footnote 55, *Leviticus Rabbah* (circa 7th century), King David says: Every day will I bless Thee; and I will praise Thy name for ever and ever. Great is the Lord, and greatly to be praised; and His greatness is unsearchable. One generation shall praise Thy works to another, and shall declare Thy mighty acts, may all flesh glorify the Lord.

God says, 'You seem to want something.'

Ψ

Does a draw happen when both teams pray for a draw? We should bring back the City Lament as a poetic form, should rescue it from football hooligans. In the absence of healthcare, the arts, education, utilities, housing . . . One really wonders what the economy's for. There are two versions of the Talmud, one written in Babylon (Bavli) and one in Palestine (Yerushalmi). In Bavli, the repentance of the Ninevites is exemplary if a little excessive (if someone built a grain silo with a single stolen brick he would destroy the whole thing to return the brick to its true owner). In Yerushalmi, the repentance is so extreme that it becomes a parody, insincere – I am nothing! I am nothing! I admired your thighs so I put out my eyes! 'Divine blackmail', Yvonne Sherwood calls it.

Ψ

Come on, you don't actually believe that, do you? It's possible that when I got back in touch I accidentally insulted you acrostically or asked for money. My apologies. My people are forced to read carefully, and write more carefully still. Through gritted teeth we speak beneath the choir. The outrage to which they hold fast, the bad narratives, when God is the god of narrative. It is what it is. When we fall back on stock phrases, corporate English, slang, we renounce belief in a larger system. We say that nothing exists other than the joke we are making, and the punchline is we're right. 'Evil' here means 'harm', it always means harm. And 'quidem' – to anticipate something by acting before it can happen.

Jonah leaves the city and goes up a hill to watch, hoping the city will be engulfed in flames, or etc. A front row seat for the annihilation. Why was he so angry? One theory goes that outside his people there *was* no prophecy, no such thing; if this was the first prophecy to really work, it stung that it should be the loathsome Ninevites who believed. Change your ways or die. These attempts to get our attention. Maybe God will spare us . . .

Ψ

In God's last dialogue with Jonah they speak exactly 39 words each. We end with a question from God, and no answer from Jonah. You cared so much about the gourd, which you didn't have any hand in making. You had feelings for the gourd. However, Jonah only cares about the gourd because it sheltered him. And God presumably knows this, but he persists. Should I not, therefore, have pity on the 120,000 people of Nineveh? And all their stuff?

Ψ

The fact that I still don't understand how the world works doesn't mean I have to like it. For our purposes Jonah is dismayed by the sudden popularity of his work. A Greatest Hits album in a cultural desert; a date with someone desperate for you, and for whom you do not care at all. Poor Laura de Noves. Cold comfort in the actual cold. If we could comprehend the night in the day, hunger in satiety. I hope the canapes were sustainably sourced.

Ψ

By this point Jonah has *twice* asked God to kill him.

Some scholars think that God does so, kills him, after the book finishes, when we're not watching. Jeez, if you insist. Or that Jonah is burned alive by the sun with no shade. Dehydrates like a strip of jerky. Which amounts to the same thing. But I don't really take that from God's tone. There's nothing to imply it. The tone He takes with Jonah is not angry or disappointed, rather bemused, detached, reasoning . . . Of course, for Jonah not to die, He'd have to send another gourd to grow in unreal time. This would also have to happen outside of the text.

Gourds

You tell me that I have given a wrong translation of some word in Jonah, and that a worthy bishop narrowly escaped losing his charge through the clamorous tumult of his people, which was caused by the different rendering of this one word. At the same time, you withhold from me what the word was which I have mistranslated; thus taking away the possibility of my saying anything in my own vindication, lest my reply should be fatal to your objection. Perhaps it is the old dispute about the gourd . . .
                     – Letter from St Jerome to St Augustine, AD 404

Jonah sits in his leafy booth on the hillside
overlooking the great city. Night comes.
He shakes like a wire. For the blanket is too narrow.
He watches to see if something acceptable will happen.

The gourd swells up from cello case to opera house,
basic stratum, basal ganglia,
politically overcommits to pleasure,
short sells luxuries, chains of sackcloth factories.

His childhood friends, at this moment –
the diplomat, the musician, the keeper of records –
sweat in their faraway offices, have minor ailments.
The Philistines control the seacoast.

He finds a little dried fish and a honeycomb
wrapped up in an ivy leaf, wrapped up in a castor oil leaf.
How did you live for eighteen years in the desert
and I cannot watch for two hours? he mutters to a Saint.

The birds brought me things.
A nice dream to be woken from by disaster.
The more powerful the vision
the more powerless the response,

rewired to pack itself away,
hiph'il for a deadly wounding,
strike, worm, strike with the alacrity
of the maggot that spoiled the manna,

the little appointment. Change one word
and it all comes tumbling down;
a single word creates a labour force;
the wealthy breathe us into being, tell the jokes

for us to live in, don't you think?
God doesn't like them, which is some relief.
This is the storm that attacked the ship;
comes in now like a heat-stripper; his feet

cook in his sandals, he rubs the dust deeper
into his eyes, the shack is scattered.
What's keeping you here?
God's wrath, which cannot be created

nor destroyed, has come to rest in him.
Are you waiting for me to tell you to go home?

Quidem

In illustrated children's books we account for the brutality
by coding God's enemies such that a child – a certain child –

would never think to question it. Priests of Baal with their throats
   slit
piled up by the river. But while they lived they had dark, pointed

evil beards; they smiled and scowled at the same time;
probably smiling about something horrible, we must surmise.

God's people implausibly Caucasian. A child from Nineveh
has been following him beyond the city walls. He wears

a little scratchy sackcloth gown. Such sights, which melt the ice
around your heart, require workers stitching through the night.

Where are you going? Leaving the city. To see what will befall it.
My city? Where are his parents? *I'm hungry.* He walks,

the child follows him. *I'm tired.* Then go home. It's dangerous here.
I'm thirsty. Take this. Not too much. Now go home. *What are you
   doing?*

Jonah erects a makeshift stall with sticks and waxy leaves. *What
   are you building?*
The child dismantles it. *Making a house?* Please go away. *Making a
   little house?*

Lord, please make this child go away. *Do you want to hear my song?*
The child sings 'Noodles in a bowl' to the tune of 'Riders on the
   Storm'.

Please. *Do you like it?* No. *Then I will cry.* The child cries. I'm sorry.
I'm sorry I said that. I liked your song. The child runs away.

Ionas Affligitur

*The ambivalence of the drama is its richness, which can
never be exhausted by prolonged acquaintance.*
                                        — Michael Marqusee

In Holbein's woodcut Jonah leans
against the gnarled trunk of a living tree —
its bark bulges like the body in a satire —
Jonah's hands are clasped together,
fingers locked under his bearded chin,
hair fashionably tousled, eyes half-closed,
his mouth distended on the right
as if snagged on a hook, the line off-stage,
my groaning is not hid from Thee
for there does not escape Thy attention one tear,
nor a quarter of a tear, nor one lambda of a tear.
His modest gown gathers at a raised knee,
looks tattered round his shoulders,
nonetheless a good fit. His sandals too,
his left foot raised on its heel,
toes point towards the city gates.
On the horizon birds (unidentifiable)
fly off in their vee. In the middle ground —
and we should pause to reflect on
just how much Jonah hates Nineveh
and how difficult it is to imply depth-
of-field in a woodcut with so few lines —

the great city smugly arrayed, some domes,
a colosseum, turrets, towers, fortified walls.
Look long enough and Jonah
seems to rock slightly, fore and aft.
Oh he will not be comforted, his promise
against Nineveh has not been fulfilled.
A bulbous cloud in the top right
resembles the dust ball of a cartoon altercation,
a fist or foot emerging now and then,
vague form of a friendly lion's face;
perhaps God. Perhaps it needed something there.
Between the stones and tufts of grass,
and just by Jonah's right leg, a large book,
open on the ground to two pages of text.
What is Jonah reading? If you think
Jonah is reading The Book of Jonah
turn back to page 1 now. Perhaps we should
look up the Bible people in the Bible read.
Perhaps it is a book of love poems
still censored for obscenity today.
Perhaps you yourself have found your name
and acts within the pages of a nameless book.
Perhaps at some point we must commit and face
whatever consequences come our way.
Perhaps Jonah's resignation is Holbein's,
reading Luther to Erasmus: 'You fancy
yourself steering more cautiously
than Ulysses between Scylla and Charybdis
as you seek to assert nothing
while appearing to assert something.'

He is Calling Elijah

Elijah finishes his story and his life beneath a juniper tree,
which is relatively easy to translate: *etz arer, wacholderbaum,*
genèvrier. Jonah reflects on the other discrepancies,
becomes increasingly enraged. Elijah was not hiding
from God but from the queen, who wanted him hanged.
Elijah wept and railed because nobody was grateful.
An actor in a pumpkin costume comes rolling up the hill
with endorsements from local celebrities on a scroll.
'Oof,' he says. 'you look like shit, man. Shouldn't
we find you somewhere shadier to lie?'
Through cloudy eyes he stares at him. Did I not
disrespect their king? he croaks.
Did I not whip the souteneurs and grind their idols underfoot?
Did I not jeer at their intellectuals, snub their awards,
spit in the faces of their billionaires?
Where are the officials baying for my blood? Where is
my fiery chariot to the stars? Where is the valedictory
pandect of human failure arrayed like tapestry?
'I don't know,' the actor says. 'We thought what you said
was pretty fair. In fact I think we need your voice more than ever.
We'll get it right next time, I guess.'
This *is* next time! Jonah sobs. Lorem ipsum,
sayeth the Lord, lorem ipsum in aeternum.

Though Like the Wanderer

During those years I was a teacher of the art of public speaking.
Love of money had gained the better of me and for it I sold to
others the means of coming off the better in debate. But you
know, Lord, that I preferred to have honest pupils, in so far as
honesty has any meaning nowadays . . .

— St Augustine, AD 397

'Well there you are. They said I'd find you here.'
Adjusts her outsized sunglasses and sits,
and balances a laptop on her knees.
'Our idea is to rebrand you as an artist, to whom
certain concessions are still granted.'
Her sack cloth gown is altered flatteringly.
If someone could just tilt him to the left . . .
His skin so rough, his mind so over-boiled
he can't be sure she isn't making sense.
'A living gift to the world. Artists needn't have any
political affiliation nor sully their imaginations
with the matters of the day — it's better that they don't.'
He crosses his eyes to double the freckle on her inner
arm. Why does anybody like him? It's almost sad.
'In the long 1990s we built a world that was a vacuum
and every part we patented and if we said it,
it was so; we had sprung into being apropos of nothing,
surveyed the scene and plugged in our guitars —
they gather dust in storage containers to this day,

we're still a little hurt by that,' she says. 'Our songs
expressed our innocence, we lived in a romantic comedy
where phones kept ringing in the background
of each scene – *will someone fucking answer that?* –
ah well. Oh well. You can't have everything.'
My people say: You can't have *anything*.
She sends the email, closes a window,
follows his gaze to the city walls and sighs.
'We want it satisfied, not quelled. The great trees
organised, not felled. A teenager without a car.
This stuff is very personal, but you're so old,
your trunk so thick, still writing of the sad tin pig,
your mind is slow, they'll kill you. The most
insulting caricature artist in the world.
How long before God says, O Useless! For O!
You are like something which resembles a bin
but is not a bin, it only looked like a bin
from a distance, so by the time people have
gone over to you and realised you are not a bin
they're annoyed to have wasted their time
and just leave their rubbish on top of you anyway.'

Bookkeeping

39 words

39

Sometimes I forget you, God admits.
Sometimes I forget the intentions I had for you,
Little keyring,
Little sparrow fob.
Until an overstuffed drawer
won't open.
Then I am forced to act.
Mutters: scit propheta . . . quod poenitentia . . .
postexilic . . . elixir . . .

39

We want. Not a colouring book nor an adventure weekend
but things that are enjoyable by accident –
which is all we really look for when we drink. *N'est pa*? Yes, pa.
Cough out your candle and come over here.

39

You need to remember the events herein
are described as they would have been seen
by a human observer were it even possible for them to be present:
In principio. To 'prink' is to make minor adjustments to yourself.

39

You look for an answer, get a play on words, it sucks
the joy out of the marrow,
knowing looks to camera.
Mishpat, justice, *Mishpach*, bloodshed.
That tracks.
I think it was Metatron we put in charge of language.

39

This was the solution to divine algebra
(if you use the spare tyre you won't have a spare tyre).
Great lengths.
And we are the carried zero,
The Absolute Undigestible.
Enduring creation or absolute justice.
You can't have both.

39

If you like you can come with me, would you like that?
God says. Still in the pumpkin patch, still on stage,
still under floorboards.
This is an effective albeit a drastic
measure to keep you out of trouble.

Previous Episodes

But night falls and it chills his sunburned limbs.
Some of the biting insects go to bed.
A woman dressed for long-haul flights
approaches over dunes. Dinah?
'Did you know that *karaoke* literally translates as *empty orchestra?*'
   she tells him.
Yes, you told me that before.
'Ah,' she says. 'I repeat myself.'
How did you know where to find me?

'Followed the trail of disappointment.'
I think I owe you an apology.
'Your problem is not even lust,' she stands over him,
'your greed is worse than that.
A woman reading next to you on a train will,
by close of journey,
be lying across your lap, murmuring in her sleep.
And that is why your visa has been refused:
that you love too many people.'

Are you a ghost? 'No, I flew in especially.
I'm on the next flight home.' She consults her notes again.
'For you are a man in a ludicrously flammable nightgown
shopping for a scented candle,' she tells him,
'a pigeon with a hood they sewed to calm him down
but forgot to ever take it off. Sex or nationalism
are ways to lose yourself within yourself,' she tells him.

You're not really here, are you? he coughs. A wild vision.
'Only Saints get those. You want my advice?'

Go home? Take care of them? he asks. She shakes her head.

'Walk down the hill and take your place in Nineveh,' she says.
'That is more or less the new covenant –
we speak here of the body literally; no country but the body and
    the mind.'
That sounds monstrous.

'It was monstrous,' she says, 'it's better now.'
She wanders out of view and he never sees her again
for the rest of his life.

It would be arrogant to think that God is trying to teach *you*
    anything, no?
You, of all people. More proper to say He's working something
    out.

Not *using* us, per se.

It's more like we're His thoughts.

Abide, Moment

They've rented him a studio in town.
A camp bed collapsed in the corner,
glass water jug with bubbles motionless.
A basket contains: one loaf, one desiccated fish.
An icon, the sole adornment on the wall,
depicts his daughters in complexly folded gowns,
sitting in their half-dismantled house.
He cannot make out their expressions from here.
His eyes aren't what they used to be a week ago.
Perhaps Little Dove is telling her sisters a story
about where he has gone. The halation
of her face more like a star. They've given him
an easel and a writing desk.
They've given him a finite time to live,
like everyone. The ceiling . . .
Why the ceiling is the underside of floorboards,
don't you think? Stalactites of dust,
thick cobwebs between the cracks,
and interrupted shafts of light. *Hello?*
A two step, three step dance keeps him awake,
which is just as well when he's got work to do.

[Abandoned canvas, streaked with tears?]

Psalm 50

Something I've been trying to articulate most of my life just
vanished again at the moment I thought I had it down, so now I'm
at the front of the queue and my hands are empty: I have no gift,
no smart clothes, no oil in my lamp, no lamp. Trying to cast my
mind backwards into last night's dream, trying to release the fish
back to the sea but they're frying on the fire; there is such a thing
as too late, mercy-as-the-ocean notwithstanding. If I were hungry,
I would not tell thee. Like writing a novel, which can bring either
glory or a decade's shame, a monumental and humiliating waste of
time, yours and everyone else's, there is no middle ground. Selah. A
voluntary pause for reflection. In the present day this may occur on
a long drive or in prison. It is not wise to pause at 3 a.m. We do not
say *selah* out loud, but honour it by pausing. I hoped by going back
into the same room, glancing in the same mirror I might recall it,
but now it feels further away than ever. It had to do with mockery,
I think, and how we set our minds aright, or think it so. Being
taught always means a stripping back to nothing first, unlearning
the wrong methods you developed to survive your own intrusive
thoughts, the right way to lift a weight heavier than you. Seeing as
thou hatest instruction. But I must find it and must tell you because
time is short and this isn't a joke, I'm being honest and I'm really
frustrated and I wanted to keep this to one page and send it to you
right away. It had to do with playing one thing off against another
to soothe ourselves, it had to do with that false comfort. But it's
been replaced by other cares. If I could only trace it back – it would

explain a lot, I think, would give us something to rekindle, I mean all of us. Ugh! I should have written it down at the time. This little pain is not enough. God says, All this I saw. And I kept silence. But soon I will shred you like an incriminating document. This has always been your final warning. Don't be so eager to be liked. Order your conversation aright. Selah, selah, selah.

Air! Air! Air!

Ah, give it all up anyway
          – Philip Guston

If there's a more dispiriting phrase than 'We invited a poet to respond . . .' I haven't heard it. God's veiny hand descending from a cloud is closed around a pink P45. To leave us smoking, eating chips in bed. The squashed-head-feeling after talking through the night. Ode to the decades you spent MONUMENTALLY DEPRESSED AND TOTALLY OUT OF FAVOUR. Hook that up to my twisty phone-line veins. A slice of pizza nailed to the wall, six hooded figures jammed into a car, the raw salami palette of the world. The days of building up to painting a single black ink line, convinced in advance of its worthlessness. That which in retrospect might be one sentence in the accompanying text on the wall of the celebratory retrospective, but at the time was half a life . . . Really how dare we be bored? But even the persecuted are bored. Jonah is emblematic of the artistic impulse refused and has to live with that. He's on the waiting list for one of several Jonah therapists but when his time arrives they send him home; can't catch a fish when you're inside the fish. At the New International Church of Jonah the readings feel a little basic. The coffee urn is set to 'slightly warm'. Centrist prayers of intercession. O comic panellist, pray to God for us. O influencer, pray to God for us. For my landlord is more working class than me. My co-eternal intermediary. A little controversial nonetheless. Your peers take one look and shake their heads: You could have had a really lovely life. You can push your self-indulgence only so far. Like a game that autosaves before a big closed door, you think *uh oh*. This must be something bad. He consults the great book of cancelled flights.

Doxology

It seems, in time, that he's the only game in town. A little dog in a little sackcloth gown. To lick my sores? To lick your sores, of course. Lots more mister nice guy, unfortunately. There is a stage show called *Young Jonah*, about his youth. Stand-up routines with variations on his prophecy, lookalikes and numerous fake accounts on social media who proffer mindless platitudes for clout. The University of Nineveh appoints a Professor of Jonah. I wonder if they'll invite you to give a talk? his new publicist thinks aloud. They don't.

In a gently lit bookshop, Jonah picks up Little Dove's novella, *Partial Eclipse*. A pink triangle on a teal background, matte finish. Oh, that's good, the bookseller says, we like that one. My daughter, he tells her. Oh! You must be very proud. This has always been the way; I had to read their poems to understand what I had done to them. Will you take a copy? He sniffs. I do not like to see myself described. Who does? There's nothing to suggest she mentions you. Do you think she might come here? says Jonah. On a book tour? He holds the book to his chest. No, there's not really much money in that anymore, the bookseller says. People don't really *go to stuff* these days, you know? People don't really do *anything* anymore – they don't listen to music or go to the theatre, they don't really ride a bike or take a walk, they take no lovers, drugs or alcohol, and if they do it does them little harm . . . On the next shelf he notices Dinah's memoir, flinches. One wonders what there is to write about, he says.

In Nineveh there are more crime writers than detectives. So easy to say it's all nonsense. So easy to say my coffee dissolves my spoon then drink it anyway. Who are we talking to and do we fear excommunication or indifference? At the Jonah writing workshop he sits towards the back. A nervous man gets to his feet, hands trembling on his loose-leaf file. He reads.

> *I hate to think of my children*
> *at my funeral,*
> *what they will wear,*
> *what they will say,*
> *about me,*
> *or about grief, generally –*

Jesus! the instructor interrupts, then *don't!* Why on earth would you think about that? Sorry, the young man says, sitting down. You don't have to put every awful thing that crosses your mind into a *poem*, she says. You can just dismiss them, the thoughts – why make yourself sad on purpose and then use that to make other people sad? No, he says, that's a good point, I see.

People have started throwing themselves off buildings in groups of seven or twenty. They don't join hands and count, they just seem to go together naturally, penguins rippling off an ice cliff. They land with awful reports. Nobody reacts. He could be walking with his publicist when a woman lands just to their right. At first Jonah is hysterical with concern, runs from body to body, checks absent pulses, shouts for blankets, cries. But soon it seems it's just the way things are. He takes coffee with the lecturer. It is a problem, isn't it? Why I'm not suffering more and others are. I don't know what to make of it *at all*. In the winter the Department of Love looks very austere in what passes for winter, passes for love. Reading anything by someone you love, he says, feels too much like staring at the sun.

Your problem, Jonah says, is you're not real. But I am. I am real. I am. Do you know, the lecturer says – he lets go of his hand – I think we'll take the narrative from here . . .

Bas Jan Ader

Art and religion degenerated as soon as they lost that comic
element which preserved us from believing that 'it happened'.
— René Daumal

What is God's attitude to art? I think
He loves it, unreservedly, all of it.
The stupid money is a manifestation of God's love,
for goodness knows it can mean little else.
In 1975, Ader walked clean through LA to his tiny boat,
a still pre-dawn, all malefactors asleep;
in the true brief off hours you can own a city,
the difference between nationhood and corporation.
I wanted to eat the light here.
This is an artist who filmed himself crying for hours
called it *I'm too sad to tell you*. I used to look
askance at the deliberate cultivation of intense feelings
but now I think it as necessary as the manufacture
of enthusiasm for your job. Some microscopic
gremlin workforce in the blood,
unbearable twinkle of a music box, the handle wound
as if a tourniquet. To put oneself in danger,
to challenge fate. What is God's attitude to tempting fate?
When Ader was / is / will be lost at sea
he left a choir singing shanties in the gallery;
I don't think they were in on it which has
worrying ethical implications. A sad maritime biography

found years later in the locker of the deceased,
a book of Jonah. But let's rejoin him on his walk,
in first gear in a low yellow car. For me,
an Englishman, it is exciting to see the Hollywood sign
in a dusty corner of a windshield; something
so self-consciously iconic, a metonym for stardom and delusion;
cigarettes and donuts; movie lots and Svengalis
and endless well-appointed homes, a body floating in the pool,
an Old Fashioned held up to a yellow moon,
world-weary voice-overs, red carpet gowns,
beauty as a classical deity. It's hard to place yourself;
you can only genuflect and touch your forehead to the ground.
Which Ader does before he steps
from the pavement to the sand. He plans
to climb into the boat and set sail, I think.
I think he's fully prepared, I don't think
he packed any supplies. There is
a long history of the attempt
to destroy the barrier between sense and nonsense.
A transgressive art, a wrong enemy,
a child describing a monster truck rally.
Now I think the way conceptual art mistrusts emotion
is suspect. I think he hurts his back
lugging the skiff into the shallows, I think
he has to stand in the water up to his knees,
look out to sea and not look back, I think.
It looks like an open book held flat
to the bridge of your nose, I think, so that
you cannot even read a single word.

The Reciprocal Trope

Little Dove buys a deck chair for the damp terrace,
ages twenty years in a single night,
smokes Marlboro Lights and gazes at the moon
and asks it if work can finally begin
after the endless relitigations? The moon winks.
It likes me, I think, she thinks.

Eventually, with no little disappointment,
we take up our vigil with the watchful and insane,
souls in full flight from their true selves.

She imagines Jonah as heraldry, mounted
on the walls of great houses converted into spas;
mindful that nothing can withstand
the patrons' militant incuriosity.

Jonah rampant on a cruise liner's poolside lounger,
rampant on a medium security prison's narrow bed,
or convalescing on the couch in shock,
like all those who were spoken to by God
and never said another word.
Spoon-feeding from a bowl of noodle soup.

Maybe he's just around the corner
in a taxi with a wheelie suitcase full of gifts for them,
and as it idles he'll emerge, swigging from a ship in a bottle.
I think I hear the car right now, in fact.

His mind will be as paintings locked in storage,
which should, by rights, belong to all of us.
A necrotic email account
rewilded by antiquated phishing scams.
I look for meaning in the detail and I don't
find it there either. I don't, it's true.

It's looking pretty bad, though, isn't it?
Can't trust – or blame – a middle manager.
May other ways hove swiftly into view;
if not for us, then the platonic you.
Her eyes have grown accustomed to the dark –
they're casting for the ever-fixèd mark.

Look, You Wouldn't Get It

One of the pleasures of listening to a lecture is to imagine yourself elsewhere. In the bar afterwards, your lover's arms, cahoots with the hysterical sunset. Had we a window you could build a house on the hills. This is also a stock-take.

Do you see [changes slide], in this Greek icon of uncertain provenance, that the whole story is depicted at once: that in the bottom left, the sailors lower Jonah by his feet to be dropped into the ocean, to be received by the great fish like communion. The great fish appears twice in the bottom-left corner, arranged like the zodiac symbol for Cancer, in a swirl like Van Gogh's 'Starry Night', swallowing Jonah from right to left and spitting him up on the shore from left to right. These are reading systems, sinistrodextral / dextrosinistral.

Many of those depicted in icons are either writing or holding open published books. This instils the questionable idea that the whole affair is somehow ennobling.

It would be good to conclude with something genuinely divinely inspired, something that does not even try. It was a Tuesday, it was every single Tuesday overlaid, when I walked down the same path to the right of the Molecular Biology department. A peculiar arrangement, of what had been planted where, and the many different substances set beneath our feet, the curl of one specific leaf, dark brown and still attached, none of it strictly intentional, as if that matters. *You are my*

God because you have no need of my goodness. I had a cold, I was behind on several references, but for the first time in my experience the act of prayer felt as natural and immediate — involuntary, in fact — as breathing in and out. On a cellular level, I mean. I was so grateful. And with this newfound power I said absolutely nothing to God and He did not reply.

NOTES

Backpfeifengesicht – a punchable face
Dépaysement – a feeling of being far from home, a change of scenery.

Roko's Basilisk refers to an online thought experiment or 'information hazard' (a theory which, to have heard of it, is to be in danger of it). Systematically debunked, it has clear resonances with Pascal's Wager; also St Herman of Alaska being admonished by a convert for converting him rather than leaving him in ignorance; and Ananias and Sapphira in the New Testament being instantly struck dead for not donating all they had to the church.

The myth of Arion is dismissed in a leather-bound concordance I have misplaced as 'unlikely to have been of any significant influence on the Book of Jonah'; I respectfully disagree.

Out of many texts consulted, the philosopher Federico Campagna's *Prophetic Culture: Recreation for Adolescents* (Bloomsbury Academic, 2021) was a continual source of delight, provocation and consolation which I cannot recommend highly enough. As was Yvonne Sherwood's electrifyingly thorough and insightful *A Biblical Text and its Afterlives: The Survival of Jonah in Western Culture* (CUP, 2001). The version of Jonah I ended up re-reading most is in Robert Alter's *Strong as Death is Love: The Song of Songs, Ruth, Esther, Jonah, Daniel – A Translation with Commentary* (W. W. Norton, 2015).

Selected further bibliography: Arnould, Elisabeth, 'The Impossible
Sacrifice of Poetry: Bataille and the Nancian Critique of Sacrifice',
Diacritics, Vol. 26, No. 2 (Summer 1996); Ellul, Jacques, *The
Judgment of Jonah*, trans. Geoffrey Bromiley, William B. Erdman
Publishing Company (Michigan, 1971); Good, Edwin M., *Irony
in the Old Testament*, The Almond Press (Sheffield, 1981);
Kugel, James L., *The Idea of Biblical Poetry: Parallelism and its
History*, Johns Hopkins Press (London, 1998); Spinoza, Baruch,
A Theologico-Political Treatise, trans. R. H. M. Elwes, Dover
Publications (New York, 1951); Wolf, Hans Walter, *Obadiah and
Jonah: A Commentary*, SPCK (London, 1986).

Bresson's *Diary of a Country Priest* (1951), based on Georges
Bernanos's novel of the same name. 'God! how is it that we fail to
recognise that the mask of pleasure, stripped of all hypocrisy, is that
of anguish?' The epigraph is a line of dialogue from the country
priest's more experienced mentor, the Priest of Torcy.

Rural parts of South Somerset and Dorset have white signposts
('fingerposts') directing the traveller to nearby villages. Some
signs at crossroads are painted bright red because, purportedly, it
was where convicted criminals used to be hanged, although this is
disputed.

Jonah does not make it to Tarshish in The Book of Jonah, which
struck me as something of a missed opportunity.

Benjamin's epigraph refers to Baudelaire's habit of insulting his
own readership in a prologue. I'm not sure my attention span is
any better than anyone else's.

Little Dove, Cosmetics Box (sometimes translated as 'Box of Eye-Shadow') and Cinnamon Flower are Job's replacement daughters, here adopted by Jonah, escaping from one allegory – on the understanding that it *is* an allegory – to another. They worry that it may not have been an allegory.

Aldous Huxley's poem 'Jonah' (1920) spends the first stanza on some gory details about the inside of a whale. My favourite couplet is 'Seated upon the convex mound / Of one vast kidney, Jonah prays . . .' (*The Collected Poetry of Aldous Huxley*, Chatto & Windus, 1971).

The anagrams (and other treated texts relating to the 'water psalm', itself an amalgamation / collage of maritime references from the Book of Psalms) are derived from Robert Alter's beautiful translation of The Book of Jonah in *Strong as Death is Love* rather than the KJV. Other references, KJV.

Momentarily obsessed with Auden's octosyllabic form in 'Under Which Lyre' but not enough to really get the hang of it. Any lines of iambic pentameter throughout should be taken as purely accidental.

My son was five years old and in Reception year at school when he told me a story about an argument taking place in the playground which developed into a fight, upon which he went off and sat on the climbing frame 'to see if something acceptable would happen'.

Many saints were fed by birds.

'He is Calling Elijah' has occasional echoes of Oscar Wilde's prose poem 'The Disciple'.

Bastiaan Johan Christiaan 'Bas Jan' Ader was a Dutch conceptual artist who disappeared in 1975. His plan was in fact to sail from Cape Cod to England so his boat was not moored in Los Angeles, but Hollywood is where the choir was, and where his journey started.

'And as for my flock, they eat that which ye have trodden with your feet; and they drink that which ye have fouled with your feet.' Ezekiel 34:19. Generally interpreted as a rebuke to authority.

My thoughts will not cater to duke or dictator is a line that appears in certain translations of a twelfth-century Silesian folk song by Dietmar Von Aist, 'Gedanke die sint ledic vri' (Only thoughts are free).

'A hero ventures forth from the world of common day into a region of supernatural wonder: fabulous forces are there encountered and a decisive victory is won: the hero comes back from this mysterious adventure with the power to bestow boons on his fellow man.' (Joseph Campbell, *The Hero With A Thousand Faces*, 1949.) The fact that I think we need to reject and move on from 'The Hero's Journey' in art and literature altogether notwithstanding, I think this is maybe where my frequent references to *baboons* comes from.

ACKNOWLEDGEMENTS

Some of these poems appeared in similar forms in *Poetry Review* and *Poetry London* over the last few years. An alternative version of 'Flat White' appears in the pamphlet *Flat White* (Periplum Press, 2023) under the title 'Milk Foam'; the text was derived from an hour-long performance lecture at the University of Plymouth's Poetry and Care conference, 2022. My thanks to Anthony Caleshu and the editors. To my colleagues at the University of Birmingham – thank you. Thank you to the Society of Authors' K Blundell Trust for a grant in 2020 which facilitated several gallery and archive visits. Big thanks to George Ttoouli for reading an early version of the manuscript. It is rare to have a friend who knows your writing's worst and best tendencies and does their best to save you from yourself (while always bearing in mind Andrew Duncan's axiom that our worst qualities may be the ones we can least afford to lose). Thank you to Colette Bryce for being an exceptionally insightful, patient, and wise editor. And thank you most of all to Holly Pester without whom this book would be even longer and almost totally without merit.